AUSCHWITZ: CREMATORIUM I
AND THE ALLEGED HOMICIDAL GASSINGS

Auschwitz: Crematorium I

and the Alleged Homicidal Gassings

Carlo Mattogno

Castle Hill Publishers
P.O. Box 243, Uckfield, TN22 9AW, UK
September 2016

HOLOCAUST HANDBOOKS, Vol. 21:
Carlo Mattogno:
Auschwitz: Crematorium I and the Alleged Homicidal Gassings.
2nd, slightly corrected and expanded edition
Translated by Henry Gardner
Uckfield, East Sussex: CASTLE HILL PUBLISHERS
P.O. Box 243, Uckfield, TN22 9AW, UK
September 2016

ISBN: 978-1-59148-968-9 (hardcover)
ISBN: 978-1-59148-156-0 (paperback)
ISSN: 1529-7748

Distribution worldwide by:
Castle Hill Publishers
P.O. Box 243
Uckfield, TN22 9AW, UK
https://shop.codoh.com

Set in Times New Roman.

www.HolocaustHandbooks.com

Cover illustrations: modern photos of: left: external view of Crematorium I at the Auschwitz Main Camp; center: morgue plus washing room in their current state; right: one of the reconstructed furnaces in the furnace hall of the crematorium; background: section of an original German blueprint of the Auschwitz Main Camp.

Table of Contents

Introduction

The orthodox history of the plan for the extermination of the Jews that was allegedly implemented at Auschwitz between 1942 and 1944 begins, as is well known, with an impalpable event: the first homicidal gassing in the basement of Block 11 of Auschwitz. This deed is said to have taken place between September 3 and 5, 1941, and to have led to the death of 250 sick detainees and 600 Soviet prisoners of war. I dedicated an in-depth study to this alleged event in 1992[1] – published in English[2] and German[3] in a revised, corrected, and enlarged edition – in which I demonstrated that this event has no historical foundation.

Orthodox historiography affirms that, because the basement of Block 11 caused too much time to be lost in ventilation, the homicidal gassings were subsequently moved to the morgue (*Leichenhalle*) of Crematorium I, the old crematorium (*altes Krematorium*) at Auschwitz, and that this space was then equipped with a ventilation device to make it suitable for such a purpose. There is, however, no trace in the documents of any such criminal use of this facility.

Initially at least, the homicidal activity, which allegedly went on in this morgue, is said to have been of an experimental nature aiming at a refinement of the method used. As in the case of the "first gassing," this activity rests entirely on testimony. In view of the total absence of documentary confirmation, this alleged milestone of the orthodox narrative of the camp was for decades relegated to the murky sidelines of historical research, generally dealt with in a few pages, if not a few lines of text.

In the present study, which is the logical sequel to *Auschwitz: The First Gassing*, I shall examine the topic of the alleged gassings in the morgue of Crematorium I from three converging viewpoints: the origin of the account and its development in the testimonies; the ventilation projects for Crematorium I and their implementation; and the material and documentary evidence.

The conclusions of this three-pronged approach, as we shall see in the chapters that follow, squarely contradict the assertions of orthodox historiography and lay bare the true nature of their shaky conjectures, which have no objective backing.

---

[1] C. Mattogno, *Auschwitz: la prima gasazione*. Edizioni di Ar, Padua, 1992.
[2] C. Mattogno, *Auschwitz: The First Gassing. Rumor and Reality*, 3rd ed., Castle Hill Publishers, Uckfield 2016.
[3] C. Mattogno, *Auschwitz: Die erste Vergasung. Gerücht und Wirklichkeit*, 2nd ed., Castle Hill Publishers, Uckfield 2014.

Chapter 1:
The Origin of the Homicidal Gassing Story

1.1. The "Gas Chamber" of Crematorium I in the Reports from the Secret Resistance Movement at Auschwitz

From April 1941 onwards, various resistance groups that had sprung up among the detainees regularly sent out detailed reports on the events in the camp, which were then collected and disseminated by the Polish government in exile in London. These reports, published by the Auschwitz Museum as a book of nearly 200 pages,[4] refer several times to rumors relating to the first alleged gassing in the basement of Block 11 − which, however, is never mentioned[5] − as well as to the alleged homicidal activity in the two provisional gas chambers at Birkenau, the so-called "Bunkers" − likewise never referred to by that name.[6]

On the other hand, these reports are practically silent about homicidal gassings which allegedly went on for a good 14 months in the morgue of Crematorium I. The crematorium of the Auschwitz camp comes up for the first time in a report dated June 1942, which merely states:[7]

"The bodies of those who die in the camp are taken to the crematorium, which can burn only 200 persons [corpses] per day, though; the remaining corpses are taken to Brzezinka [Birkenau] and buried in graves dug for that purpose. The corpses of those who have been gassed are also buried there."

The next reference to the crematorium is contained in a "letter written from the Auschwitz camp" dated August 29, 1942:[8]

"Every day, two fully loaded carts, which contain some 150 persons [corpses], go to the crematorium, which has been enlarged and remodeled to absorb 200 persons [corpses] in 24 hours."

---

[4]   "Obóz koncentracyjny Oświęcim w świetle akt Delegatury Rządu R.P. na Kraj" (The Auschwitz Concentration Camp in the Light of the Proceedings of the Delegatura of the Polish Government in Exile), *Zeszyty oświęcimskie*, special no. I, Wydawnictwo Państwowego Muzeum w Oświęcimiu, 1968.

[5]   *Ibid.*, pp. 11, 15, 16, 52, 67. Cf. C. Mattogno, *op. cit.* (note 2), pp. 31-36.

[6]   Cf. in this respect my study *Debunking the Bunkers of Auschwitz: Black Propaganda versus History*, 2nd ed., Castle Hill Publishers, Uckfield 2016.

[7]   "Obóz koncentracyjny…," *op. cit.* (note 4), p. 34. The last sentence refers to the alleged temporary gas chambers of Birkenau.

[8]   *Ibid.*, p. 42.

The "Memorandum on the situation in the country for the period of October 11 through November 15, 1942" gives the following information:[9]

> *"The official book of the detainees who have been burnt so far in the crematoria*[10] *of Auschwitz lists as of August 15 some 18,800*[11] *surnames of martyrs for this camp. Not mentioned in this book are the tens of thousands who are sent to Auschwitz merely for the purpose of being exterminated there immediately in the gas chambers* [w komarach gazowych]. *"*

The only reference to the alleged gas chamber in Crematorium I appears in a report of November 1942:[12]

> *"There are two poisoning sites: in the camp crematorium (capacity 400 persons) and at Brzezinka* [Birkenau], *where several considerably larger houses near the forest have been converted for this purpose."*

Surprisingly, for the 14 months of the operation of the "gas chamber" in Crematorium I, where several tens of thousands of people are said to have perished, no detainee in the camp noted anything, and the "truth" was discovered by the resistance movement of the camp only a few weeks before such activity allegedly ended!

1.2. Origin and Development of the Official Version

Between February 14 and March 8, 1945, an investigative Commission consisting of the Poles R. Dawidowski and J. Doliński as well as the Soviet citizens V.F. Lavrushin and A.M. Schuer drew up a report on the "gas chambers" and the crematoria of Auschwitz-Birkenau, which contains the following passage on Crematorium I:[13]

> *"In early 1941, a crematorium, designated as Crematorium #1, was started up in the Auschwitz camp. It had two furnaces with two muffles each, heated by four coke gasifiers. At the end of 1941, in September or October,*[14] *a third furnace with 2 muffles of the same type as the first two was set up in the same place* [the furnace room]. *Each muffle could accommodate 3 to 5 corpses at one time, cremation lasted one hour and a half, and the number of corpses cremated amounted to 300 to 350 per day.*

---

[9] "Obóz koncentracyjny...," *op. cit.* (note 4), p. 56. The report is dated November 15, 1942.

[10] *"w krematoriach;"* as is well known, at that time there existed only one crematorium, the one at the Main Camp (*Stammlager*).

[11] The accuracy of this figure cannot be verified, because the registers of the cremations have not been preserved.

[12] "Obóz koncentracyjny...," *op. cit.* (note 4), p. 69.

[13] GARF, 7021-108-15, pp. 2f. This report exists in a number of copies.

[14] The date is in error, Cf. Chapter 5.3.

Next to this crematorium there was a gas chamber, which had, at either end, gas-tight doors with peep-holes and in the ceiling four openings with hermetic closures through which the 'Ziklon' for the killing of the persons was thrown. Crematorium I operated until March 1943 and existed in that form for two years."

On the basis of rather fanciful assumptions (an operational period of 14 months, an activity coefficient of 0.5 and a monthly capacity of 9,000 corpses), the experts then calculated a total of 63,000 corpses as having been cremated,[15] but did not specify whether these were victims of the alleged gas chamber.

The description was very terse, because the Soviets had not yet found either witnesses or documents regarding the homicidal use of the crematorium. Such a use was evidently assumed on account of the three gas-tight doors (*Gasschutztüren*), which, as we shall see in Chapter 6, had been installed in late 1944, when the crematorium was converted to an "air-raid shelter for the SS hospital with operating room" (*Luftschutzbunker für SS-Revier mit einem Operationsraum*). This is confirmed by the fact that, in its original state, the morgue did in fact have two doors, but not "at either end." That was the case in the February to March 1945 period.

The serious gaps of the Soviet Commission were only partially filled a few months later by a Polish detainee, Stanisław Jankowski (see Chapter 3.1.). He created the literary basis of the story about gassings in Crematorium I, which, however, went nearly unnoticed by interrogators and historians alike.

On September 26, 1946, at the request of Jan Sehn, the investigating judge in the trial of Rudolf Höss (March 11-29, 1947) and that of the Auschwitz camp garrison (November 25 to December 16, 1947), the engineer Roman Dawidowski drew up a lengthy technical opinion on the alleged extermination installations at Auschwitz-Birkenau. On the subject of criminal activity in Crematorium I, this expert wrote:[16]

"One now began to poison people regularly with Zyklon B and to use for that purpose the Leichenhalle (morgue) of Crematorium I (photograph 18).[17] This chamber had a floor area of 65 square meters – 17 by 4.5 meters[18] – and on both sides had a gas-tight door. Gassing took place by dumping the contents of Zyklon cans through openings in the ceiling."

The opinion states furthermore that from March 1942 onwards thousands of Jews arrived at Auschwitz every day and that "the gas chamber of

---

[15]　*Ibid.*, p. 19.
[16]　AGK, NTN, 93; Höss trial, vol. 11, pp. 26f.
[17]　This concerns the plan of Crematorium I, Topf D 59042, of September 25, 1941. Cf. Document 3 in the appendix.
[18]　Calculation error: 17×4.5=76.5. The morgue measured 17×4.6=78.2 m².

Crematorium I turned out to be inadequate for their liquidation." The alleged gassings were, therefore, moved to the so-called "Bunkers" of Birkenau.

Toward the end of 1946, Jan Sehn summarized the results of this research in a long article entitled "The Auschwitz Concentration and Extermination Camp."[19] In the chapter on the "gas chambers," he simply included the corresponding passage from Roman Dawidowski's opinion, including the error about the floor area, and adding the mistake of the Soviet experts with respect to the position of the gas-tight doors:[20]

> *"From there on, subsequent gassings took place in the gas chamber of Crematorium I. This chamber had a floor area of 65 square meters and a gas-tight door at either end. Gassing was effected by dumping through openings in the ceiling the contents of the cans, which gave off a toxic gas. From that time on, gassing of persons increased systematically."*

Also in 1946, Filip Friedman, director of the "Jewish Historical Commission in Poland," published a book on Auschwitz, "compiled from official records and evidence and eyewitness accounts," in which he writes the following:[21]

> *"The same year* [1941] *permanent gas installations were installed in two peasant huts at Brzezinki (Birkenau). The bodies of the gassed people were buried near the huts. By the spring of 1942, the bodies began to rot and smell, and steps were taken to build a crematorium in which to burn the corpses. This was the origin of the first small crematorium with a gas chamber at Oswiecim. It was, however, still only an improvisation on a small scale."*

Thus, inverting the actual sequence of events according to orthodox historiography, he has the so-called "Bunkers" at Birkenau come into being in 1941[22] and makes the installation of Crematorium I a subsequent event.

The written verdict of the Höss trial (April 2, 1947) devotes less than one line to the problem of alleged homicidal gassings in Crematorium I:[23]

> *"Gassing of detainees was introduced in the area of this camp in 1941, initially in the basement of Block 11, later in the morgue of Crematorium I* [...]. *"*

The indictment in the trial of the Auschwitz camp garrison (November 1947) was just as laconic in this regard:[24]

---

[19] Jan Sehn, "Obóz koncentracyjny i zagłady Oświęcim," in: *Biuletyn Głównej Komisji Badania Zbrodni Niemieckich w Polsce,* vol. I, Poznań 1946, pp. 63-130.

[20] *Ibid.*, p. 121.

[21] F. Friedman, *This Was Oswiecim. The History of a Murder Camp*, The United Jewish Relief Appeal, London 1946, pp. 18f.

[22] According to the orthodox historiography, "Bunker 1" went into service in March or May 1942, "Bunker 2" in June 1942.

[23] AGK, NTN, 146z, p. 31.

[24] RGVA, 7021-108-39, p. 37.

"Then the gassings took place in a special chamber in Crematorium I, and later also in the so-called Bunkers 1 and 2 at Birkenau, in farmhouses, whose inhabitants had been removed."

In 1949, Bruno Baum, an ex-detainee of Auschwitz who had organized the German resistance group, published a book specifically dedicated to the camp resistance. As such, Baum was no doubt one of the best-informed former inmates about events in the camp, but still, regarding the alleged gassings in Crematorium I, he had nothing better to say than the few lines that follow:[25]

"One day, the news spread that in the old crematorium of the Main Camp they had tried to kill detainees by means of gas. This information was soon confirmed."

And that is all.

When the Central Commission for the Investigation of Hitlerian Crimes in Poland published a Polish-language edition of the so-called memoirs of Rudolf Höss in 1956,[26] historians, who so far suffered from a lack of information about the claimed gassings in Crematorium I, had now access to the statements of the Auschwitz commandant.

Together with the "report" by Pery Broad – drawn up on July 13, 1945, then lost, later miraculously rediscovered for the Frankfurt Auschwitz trial (December 20, 1963, to August 20, 1965), but not in its original form, of which no one knows the whereabouts – the Höss paper became the keystone of the evidence concerning the claimed reality of homicidal gassings in Crematorium I and would invariably be referred to in the orthodox literature.

The year 1958 saw the publication of the German version of a book written by Ota Kraus and Erich Kulka, which had first been published in 1946. It claimed to be a detailed history of the Auschwitz camp, entitled *The Factory of Death (Die Todesfabrik)*. In the chapter dealing with "the first gassing experiments" (*die ersten Vergasungsversuche*), the authors make the following rather terse remarks:[27]

"The first mass gassing of transports at Auschwitz took place in early 1942 in the only crematorium then available at the Auschwitz I concentration camp. Prior to that, physically weak detainees, mainly Russian POWs, had been killed in smaller groups by means of gas.

The Auschwitz crematorium was small. It had a gas chamber for 600 to 800 persons and six cremation furnaces.

[25] B. Baum, *Widerstand in Auschwitz. Bericht der internationalen antifaschistischen Lagerleitung*, VVN-Verlag, Berlin-Potsdam 1949, p. 11.

[26] Central Commission for the Investigation of Hitlerian Crimes in Poland (ed.), *Wspomnienia Rudolfa Hössa komendanta obozu oświęmciskiego*, Wydawnictwo Prawnicze, Warsaw 1956.

[27] O. Kraus, E. Kulka, *Die Todesfabrik*, Kongress-Verlag, Berlin 1958, p. 110.

A further victim of mass execution by gas was the transport of Slovak Jews from Zilina in May 1942. This gassing was not yet carried out in such a cunning way as was the case a few days later, after Himmler's visit.
Once the first test had been successful, they started building four large crematoria with gas chambers at Birkenau."

Otherwise, Kraus and Kulka relied on Höss's declarations.[28] The claim about the gassing of the Slovak transport had been taken from a statement by Filip Müller (see Chapter 3.3.). The errors in the interpretation (the reason for building the Birkenau crematoria) and in the sequence of events (Himmler's visit took place in July 1942, not in May) reflect the uncertainty of the historical knowledge at the time.

Even in the 1960s, Jan Sehn, in his book on Auschwitz, deals with the question of the alleged gas chamber of Crematorium I in only a couple of lines, the same as those of his 1946 article:[29]

"The mortuary (Leichenkeller)[30] of the first Oswiecim crematorium – used for gassing after the first test in Block 11 – was 65 sq. m. in area and was fitted with two gas-proof doors. Cyclon was thrown in through openings in the ceiling. From 1942 on, mass transports of Jews began to arrive at Oswiecim. The gas chamber of Crematorium I proved inadequate for their liquidation."

In one of the first general accounts of the camp's history published by the Auschwitz Museum, the page Franciszek Piper devoted to Crematorium I is based on only one source: the "memoirs" of Rudolf Höss![31]

Another testimony considered essential and immediately absorbed by orthodox historiography appeared in 1979: the author, Filip Müller, asserted he had worked for 16 months in Crematorium I at Auschwitz, from May 1942 until July 1943.[32]

In 1989, Danuta Czech, in the second German edition of her Auschwitz *Kalendarium*, attempted to historicize the story of gassings in Crematorium I at Auschwitz by giving precise indications regarding the beginnings of the alleged homicidal activity. The value of her entries will be examined in Chapter 4.1.

Jean-Claude Pressac was the first scholar to try to bring the vagaries of the accounts surrounding the homicidal gassings in the morgue of Crematorium I into a historical framework. In 1989 he devoted a whole chapter of

[28] *Ibid.*, pp. 110f.
[29] Jan Sehn, *Oświęcim-Brzezinka (Auschwitz-Birkenau) Concentration camp*, Wydawnictwo Prawnicze, Warsaw 1961, p. 125.
[30] Wrong term, properly used only for the semi-basement morgues of Crematoria II and III at Birkenau.
[31] F. Piper, "Extermination," in: State Museum Auschwitz (ed.), *Auschwitz (Oświęcim) Camp hitlérien d'extermination*, Editions Interpress, Warsaw 1978, p. 118.
[32] Filip Müller, *Sonderbehandlung. Drei Jahre in den Krematorien und Gaskammern von Auschwitz*, Verlag Steinhausen, Munich 1979; Müller's statements will be examined in Chapter 3.3.

his first book to this question, in which he attempted to demonstrate the historical reality of the homicidal gassings in Crematorium I on the basis of mere testimony.[33]

In his second book, which appeared four years later,[34] Pressac claims ambitiously to furnish documentary evidence for the use of the morgue of Crematorium I as a homicidal gas chamber. His theses will be evaluated in depth in Chapter 5.

The most penetrating – or, more precisely, the least superficial – official study of the alleged homicidal gas chamber of Crematorium I at Auschwitz is contained in the section "Krematorium I" of the chapter "The Methods of Annihilation," written by Franciszek Piper, which is part of the most comprehensive work on this camp published by the Auschwitz Museum.[35] We are dealing here with a little more than ten pages of text accompanied by four pages of drawings and photographs. Two and a half pages summarizing this section had already appeared in English in 1994.[36]

According to this study, which represents the peak of orthodox historiography on this topic, the gas chamber operated from September 1941 until early December 1943 and was instrumental in the deaths of "several tens of thousands" of Jewish victims.[37]

David Irving discovered the verbatim interrogation protocol of SS-*Hauptsturmführer* Hans Aumeier by the British authorities after his arrest on June 11, 1945. Aumeier had been assigned to Auschwitz in 1942 and 1943. These documents have been cited by orthodox historians as confirmation – or "converging evidence" – of the reality of homicidal gassings in Crematorium I at Auschwitz. I shall deal with this claim in Chapter 3.4.

Before any detailed examination of the rare testimonies on the alleged homicidal activities in the morgue of Crematorium I can be undertaken, it is indispensable to establish the documentary framework of what is historically certain about this installation. Regarding the history of the cremation

---

[33] J.-C. Pressac, *Auschwitz: Technique and operation of the gas chambers*, The Beate Klarsfeld Foundation, New York 1989. The chapter is on pp. 123-159.

[34] J.-C. Pressac, *Les crématoires d'Auschwitz. La machinerie du meurtre de masse*, CNRS Editions, Paris 1993; German: *Die Krematorien von Auschwitz. Die Technik des Massenmordes*, Piper, Munich, Zürich 1994. Subsequent page numbers refer to the French original.

[35] Wacław Długoborski, Franciszek Piper (eds.), *Auschwitz 1940-1945. Węzłowe zagadnienia z dziejów obozu*. Wydawnictwo Państwowego Muzeum Oświęcim-Brzezinka, 1995, vol. III, *Zagłada*, pp. 102-113. English version: *Auschwitz 1940-1945. Central Issues in the History of the Camp*, Auschwitz-Birkenau State Museum 2000, vol. III, pp. 121-133.

[36] F. Piper, "Crematorium I," paragraph of paper "Gas Chambers and Crematoria," in: I. Gutman, M. Berenbaum (eds.), *Anatomy of the Auschwitz Death Camp*, Indiana University Press, Bloomington/Indianapolis 1994, pp. 158-160.

[37] *Ibid.*, p. 160.

equipment, I refer the reader to the detailed discussion I have presented elsewhere.[38]

In the following chapter, I shall mainly focus on the ventilation devices for the morgue – planned and realized – and on the changes that the crematorium went through in November 1944. In Chapter 6 I will return to this latter point when dealing with the modifications to which the crematorium was subjected by the Polish authorities in 1946 and 1947.

---

[38] C. Mattogno, F. Deana, *The Cremation Furnaces of Auschwitz: A Technical and Historical Study*, Castle Hill Publishers, Uckfield 2015, Vol. I, Part II, Chapter 6.1.

Chapter 2:
Crematorium I at Auschwitz

2.1. The Projects for the Ventilation System of Crematorium I

The correspondence between the SS-*Neubauleitung* (New Construction Office, later *Bauleitung* = Construction Office, finally *Zentralbauleitung* = Central Construction Office) in Auschwitz and the Erfurt company Topf & Söhne contains many documents concerning the projects for ventilating Crematorium I. The first reference appears in a letter from Topf dated December 9, 1940, on the subject of "ventilation system for morgue cells (*Leichenzellen*) and dissecting room, our offer 40/1096." Topf indicates that for the dissecting room 10 exchanges of air per hour had been provided for, and 20 for the "morgue." The fresh air for the morgue would be made available by windows or other openings:[39]

> "*For the removal of the exhaust air we recommend a brick chimney with a minimum height of 10 m above ground.*"

The equipment could be supplied within three months. As an attachment, the letter contained Topf drawing D 57999 showing the location of the ducts and of the fan. The corresponding cost estimate (*Kosten-Anschlag*), dated December 9, 1940, also attached to the letter mentioned, amounted to 1,784 RM. Topf offered a fan, No. 450,[40] for the extraction of 6,000 normal cubic meters[41] of air per hour against a total pressure difference of 25 mm of water column, driven by a three-phase electric motor of 1.5 horsepower. The exhaust duct (*Abluft-Rohrleitung*) went from the dissecting room (*Sezierraum*) to the fan installed in the morgue and had a diameter rising from 180 to 450 millimeters.[42]

At the time, the morgue was L-shaped and extended to the rear of the second furnace, as is clear from drawing 57999 of November 30, 1940, which, however, does not show the ventilation equipment (cf. Document

---

[39] RGVA, 502-1-312, pp. 136f.; "*Für die Abführung der Abluft empfehlen wir einen gemauerten Kamin mit einer Mindesthöhe von 10 m über Erdoberfläche.*"

[40] The figure indicated the diameter (in millimeters) of the duct linked to the blower.

[41] Referring to air under "normal" conditions.

[42] "*Kosten-Anschlag*" by Topf of December 9, 1940, re. "*Entlüftungs-Anlage für Leichenzellen und Sezierraum*". RGVA, 502-1-312, S. 138-140; cf. Document 6.

1). The latter was probably laid out as shown in J.-C. Pressac's drawing:[43] the chimney was to go up along the wall separating the morgue from the coke storage room, with the fan being mounted in front of it and the ducts from the dissecting room and the morgue running along the sidewalls of the crematorium. Pressac's drawing contains, however, a serious error in the sense that he misinterprets the Topf letter of December 9, 1940, saying "a 10-fold [...] and 20-fold exchange of air" per hour for the dissecting room and the morgue, respectively. Instead, Pressac reads "10 air-intake ports"[44] for the former and "20 air-intake ports" for the latter, which he has painstakingly added to the pipework in his drawing!

On January 21, 1941, head of construction August Schlachter informed Topf of certain changes in the crematorium building:[45]

"On account of the creation of an urn storage room, the morgue changes its layout, as shown in blue in the drawing.
The fan with its motor is to be placed in the urn room. The creation of the urn room leads to the change in the design of the air extraction equipment. Moreover, it is desired to attach the furnace hall to the ventilation system."

On February 3, 1941, Topf drew up another cost estimate for "1 ventilation system for corpse and dissecting room, 1 ventilation system for furnace room" for a total cost of 2,486 RM. The equipment for the dissecting room and the morgue was the same as before. In addition, there was a blower No. 300 of 3,000 cubic meters per hour against a pressure of 15 mm of water column, driven by a 0.75 HP three-phase electric motor, for the furnace hall. The corresponding ducts started in the center of the hall and had a section increasing from 255 to 300 millimeters.[46] The design probably corresponded to J.-C. Pressac's drawing:[47] the two blowers stood in the urn room and were connected to a brick chimney rising from this room.

---

[43] J.-C. Pressac, *op. cit.* (note 34), p. 17. Cf. J.-C. Pressac, Robert J. van Pelt, "The Machinery of Mass Murder at Auschwitz," in I. Gutman, M. Berenbaum (eds.), *op. cit.* (note 36), p. 194.
[44] In the original: "dix et vingt prises d'air." J.-C. Pressac, *op. cit.* (note 34), p. 18. In "The Machinery of Mass Murder at Auschwitz," (note 43), this passage is missing, but the mistake appears in the legend of the corresponding drawing, which speaks of "10 air exchangers" and "20 air exchangers" (p. 194).
[45] RGVA, 502-1-327, p. 185.
[46] "*1 Entlüftungs-Anlage für Leichen- und Sezier-Raum, 1 Entlüftungs-Anlage für Ofen-Raum,*" RGVA, 502-1-312, pp. 123-126. Cf. Document 7.
[47] J.-C. Pressac, *op. cit.* (note 34), p. 19. Cf. J.-C. Pressac, R.J. van Pelt *op. cit.* (note 43), p. 195. In this drawing, the ventilation duct of the morgue runs along the opposite wall as compared to the first drawing and is thus shorter. Pressac has probably noticed that the price for the duct in the first cost estimate was 924 RM, as against 867 RM in the second one, and may have deduced from this a shorter length of the duct.

On February 15, 1941, Schlachter informed Topf that he did not want a ventilation chimney. The design would have to be changed with the exhaust air now feeding into the existing chimney.[48]

Topf worked out a third estimate in accordance with the wishes of the SS-*Neubauleitung*, dated February 24, 1941.[49] The design is shown in drawing D 58052 of the same date.[50] The equipment consisted of a blower No. 550 – with a capacity of 8,600 cubic meters per hour driven by a three-phase electric motor of 3 HP – placed to the right of the chimney. The duct had an initial cross section of 550 mm and split into three smaller branches, which went to the dissecting room, the furnace hall, and the morgue. Total cost was 1,884 RM plus 596 RM for the installation. Delivery was to be within six months.

On March 15, 1941, the SS-*Neubauleitung* placed the order based on the estimate of February 24, and on March 24 Topf officially confirmed it.[51] However, since the delivery time was very long, Schlachter ordered a temporary ventilation system to be installed in the crematorium at the end of February. In his "activity report" of March 1, 1941, for the period of February 23 to March 1, 1941, he wrote:[52]

"in the crematorium, the work on the new incineration plant has been terminated, a temporary ventilation has been connected to the exhaust channel, and everything has been overhauled."

The "exhaust channel" (*Abzugskanal*) was the flue of the first crematorium furnace.

On June 7, 1941, SS-*Untersturmführer* Maximilian Grabner, head of the Auschwitz Political Department, wrote the following letter to SS-*Neubauleitung*:[53]

"It is absolutely necessary to install a separate ventilation in the morgue of the crematorium. The existing ventilation has been rendered useless by the installation of the second furnace. When the second furnace is in use – and that is now the case almost daily – the ventilation flap to the morgue has to be closed because otherwise warm air enters the morgue through the flue, causing the exact opposite of a ventilation.
The deficiencies of the ventilation and of the fresh air feed are particularly noticeable under the prevailing conditions of warm weather. It is hardly possible

---

[48] RGVA, 502-1-312, p. 121.
[49] RGVA, 502-1-327, pp. 195-197. Cf. Document 8.
[50] *"Entlüftungsanlage,"* RGVA, 502-1-327, pp. 191f. Cf. Document 2.
[51] RGVA, 502-1-312, p. 118.
[52] *"Im Krematorium wurden die Arbeiten für die neue Verbrennungsanlage fertiggestellt, eine provisorische Entlüftung an den Abzugskanal angeschlossen und alles instandgesetzt,"* RGVA, 502-1-214, p. 67.
[53] RGVA, 502-1-312, p. 111. Cf. Document 9.

to spend any time in the morgue, even if such instances are generally of short duration.

A proper ventilation will surely lead to an improvement in the quality of the air and to a reduction of the humidity of the room. It would also do away with the presence of flies in the morgue or at least reduce this nuisance to a minimum.

The elimination of such deficiencies is in the general interest, not least because it would put a stop to the spread of disease by the flies. It is therefore requested that two ventilators be installed in the morgue, one for feeding fresh air and one for ventilation. A separate duct leading to the chimney must be provided for the ventilation. It is requested that the work be started as soon as possible."

The temporary ventilation of the morgue had been installed during the construction of the second crematorium furnace by connecting its left-side flue – which ran along the partition between the furnace hall and the morgue – to the latter room (see Documents 10 and 11).

The system's functioning depended on the chimney's draft, which, by lowering the pressure in the flue, also sucked in air from the morgue. The system worked well only when exclusively the first furnace was in operation, the two flues[54] of which were far enough away from the ventilation duct of the morgue.[55] When, however, the second furnace came into regular use – "almost daily," says Grabner – the hot gases from the muffle on the left, on entering the respective flue, immediately reached the ventilation duct. If the flap of that duct was open, a portion of the gases entered the morgue, warming it up.

Grabner hence requests the installation of two blowers in the morgue, one for fresh air, one for the exhaust air, and the construction of a separate conduit to the chimney. The German term used – *"Fuchs"* – designates a flue between the furnace and the chimney, because Grabner was aiming for a brick duct that would pass under the floor of the furnace hall.

Between the end of September and the middle of October 1941, ventilation work, which certainly stemmed from Grabner's complaints, was carried out in the crematorium. A "work sheet" of the inmate locksmith shop dated September 25, 1941, mentions the following order: "Make 4 air-tight flaps." The work was done the same day by the detainees Zalewski (8363),

---

[54] Each muffle of the two furnaces had a lateral flue linking up with the main flue, which ran below the paved floor in front of the furnaces up to the chimney, as illustrated in Document 10.

[55] In the beginning, the second furnace was not often used, either because it still had to dry out, or because in early April draft problems became apparent. On April 2, 1941, Schlachter sent Topf a telegram and a letter to inform them that "the 2nd furnace unit has too little draft, which prevents the cremation from being carried out to completion" (*"die 2. Ofenanlage zu wenig Zug hat, sodass die Verbrennung nicht vollkommen durchgeführt werden kann"*); RGVA, 502-1-312, p. 113. Topf gave instructions to SS-Neubauleitung on how to solve the problem in a letter which bears the same date; RGVA, 502-1-312, pp. 115f.

Morgiel (7868), and Dudziński (16197), blacksmiths, and Bialas (1461), welder, in a total of 11 man-hours. As is noted on the back of the sheet, the 4 flaps were done in black plate (*Schwarzblech*).[56]

Another work sheet of the inmate locksmith shop for the crematorium, established October 7, 1941,[57] refers to "fabrication of 2 ventilation caps in steel plate with an internal length of 27/27 cm, otherwise according to instructions." The work was done by the detainee welder Bialas and the detainee plumbers Maliszewski (9612) and Dyntar (1409) in a total of 50 man-hours between October 7 and 13, 1941. For the fabrication of these devices, 4 square meters of black plate were used.[58]

The "air-tight flaps" were air-tight closures which served to block off the ducts of a room from the system of ventilation. The "ventilation caps" were probably vertical tubes with caps for ventilation, similar to those (in brickwork) which were erected on the roof of the crematorium above the two furnaces for the ventilation of the furnace room.

The "Inventory map of building No. 47a, BW 11, crematorium," drawn on April 10, 1942 by detainee 20033 (the Polish engineer Stefan Swiszczowski), shows in its view of the chimney on the flat roof, to the left, a thick angled tube, which probably housed an intake fan (*Belüftung*).[59] It could not have been an exhaust fan (*Entlüftung*) or a duct for exhaust air for two reasons: first of all, for the evacuation of the waste air from the morgue, Topf had proposed a chimney 10 meters high, whereas the SS-*Neubauleitung*, for reasons of economy, had opted for the use of the existing chimney. Both Topf and SS-*Neubauleitung* were in agreement that the air removed from an ordinary morgue would have to be discharged at least 10 meters above ground. In that case, how could SS-*Neubauleitung* have decided to discharge not only the waste air from the morgue but even the lethal exhaust from the alleged homicidal gas chamber through a duct no more than 5 feet high?

Secondly, blowing out the waste air through the duct in question would have necessitated opening one or both doors of the morgue – not a good solution hygienically for an ordinary morgue, and highly dangerous for a homicidal gas chamber.

Hence, if an intake fan had been housed in that duct, the ventilation of the morgue could only have been of the type requested by Grabner. The ventilation system of the morgue was connected, through a metal duct, to the smoke flue that passed under the floor of the furnace room and went to

---

[56] RGVA, 502-2-1, pp. 74-74a. Cf. Document 12
[57] The date refers to the receipt of the order.
[58] RGVA, 502-2-1, pp. 75-75a. Cf. Document 13.
[59] "*Bestandplan des Gebäudes Nr. 47a B.W. 11, Krematorium*," RGVA, 502-2-146, p. 21. Cf. Document 4.

the chimney. Upstream of the flue's juncture with the chimney there was an exhaust fan.

Such an arrangement, however, could have functioned only until early July 1942, when the old chimney of the crematorium was demolished. No air conduit was, in fact, attached to the new chimney, as is evident from the corresponding design drawing done by the Köhler company on August 11, 1942.[60]

The ventilation equipment Topf had supplied in late 1941 on the basis of the estimate submitted on February 24, 1941, was never installed and rusted away in a warehouse.

On October 28, 1942, Topf sent the Central Construction Office at Auschwitz drawing no. D 58052, which they had already dispatched to the SS-*Neubauleitung* on February 24, 1941 with the following comment:[61]

"We also attach drawing D 58052 of the ventilation system still to be installed for the furnace system of the old Crematorium I Kl. that we supplied years ago."

On November 27, 1942, SS-*Untersturmführer* Fritz Wolter wrote a memo concerning "Ventilations for crematoria" (*Entlüftungen für Krematorien*):[62]

"On November 27, 1942, the undersigned had a telephone conversation with engineer Prüfer of Topf & Sohn, Erfurt. The company would have a fitter available in a week's time. He would set up the ventilation system, if the roofs of the special cellars are ready; also the forced draft for the five 3-muffle furnaces.

At the same time, the ventilation system could be installed in the old crematorium."

A postscript specifies that, after discussion with SS-*Untersturmführer* Janisch, the Topf fitter could start the job in three weeks' time. On November 30, Topf, referring to "Crematorium,[63] aeration and de-aeration system," inquired about the urgency of the matter.[64] SS-*Hauptsturmführer* Bischoff, head of the Central Construction Office, advised Topf the same day as follows:[65]

"The fitter you offered can start <u>immediately</u> with the installation of the ventilation system in the <u>old</u> crematorium at Auschwitz concentration camp. After completion of this job, the forced draft system for Crematorium I [= II] (five 3-muffle furnaces) in the POW camp can be installed."

---

[60] *"Rauchkanal für die Zentral-Bauleitung der Waffen-SS und Polizei Auschwitz O.S.,"* RGVA, 502-2-23, p. 18.
[61] APMO, BW 30/34, p. 96.
[62] RGVA, 502-1-313, p. 65.
[63] It concerned the future Crematorium II of the Birkenau camp.
[64] RGVA, 502-1-313, p. 62.
[65] RGVA, 502-1-314, p. 17.

As the last point, Bischoff then requested the ventilation system for Crematorium II to be installed.

In a list of invoices, which the Central Construction Office had not yet paid, there is also an invoice concerning the ventilation system of Crematorium I in an amount of 1,884 RM,[66] based on the cost estimate of February 24, 1941. The equipment had, therefore, been delivered by Topf, but there is no document proving that it was actually installed in the old crematorium as "immediately" requested by Bischoff.

Crematorium I almost certainly stopped its activity on July 17, 1943, as shown by a letter written the previous day by Bischoff to the head of SS garrison administration, SS-*Sturmbannführer* Möckel, on the need to take the plant out of service because of the fire hazard it posed to the two wooden barracks of the Political Department constructed next to it.[67]

2.2. The Transformation of Crematorium I into an Air-Raid Shelter

On November 16, 1943, the commandant of the Auschwitz camp, SS-*Obersturmbannführer* Liebehenschel, issued the following order regarding "Air-raid measures at garrison Auschwitz":[68]

> "Upon advice of the superior authorities in charge, the necessary air-raid protection measures will now also be undertaken in the Auschwitz garrison area with immediate effect. In my quality as the local air-raid protection officer in charge, I have appointed SS-Untersturmführer Josten to be my permanent representative. I request all services to support SS-Untersturmführer Josten in every possible way."

The order became effective as of January 1, 1944.[69] According to the usual practice, a construction site was defined for this purpose: BW 98, "air-raid shelter trench," into which all such shelters planned or eventually built at Auschwitz were integrated. They became sections of BW 98, and carried the same designation, with an added letter. For example, the air-raid shelter of the camp commandant's residence became BW 98J. The old crematorium at Auschwitz also became part of this system of air-raid protection measures.

---

[66] *"43/314 Entlüftungs-Anlage für Krem. I, Rechnung v. 27.5.43,"* RGVA, 502-1-313, p. 26.
[67] RGVA, 502-1-324, p. 1.
[68] Standortbefehl Nr. 51/43 of November 16, 1943. GARF, 7021-108-32, p. 73.
[69] Letter of the camp commandant SS-*Obersturmbannführer* Liebehenschel in his function of *"Der SS-Standortälteste als örtlicher Luftschutzleiter"* (senior garrison officer as local air-raid protection chief) to Zentralbauleitung of February 17, 1944. RGVA, 502-1-401, p. 100.

On July 16, 1944, during his visit to Auschwitz, SS-*Obergruppenführer* Pohl approved the "Installation of a gas-proof operating room and shrapnel-proof shelter in the former crematorium for the garrison surgeon," which became BW 98M.[70]

On August 26, 1944, Josten, who had meanwhile been promoted to SS-*Obersturmführer* and appointed "head of air-raid protection," wrote a letter to the camp commandant on "conversion of the old crematorium for air-raid protection purposes," which reads as follows:[71]

> *"In the attachment I submit a project for the conversion of the old crematorium for air-raid protection purposes with the request for approval of this transformation.*
>
> *1. Work scheduled:*
> *Dismantling of the old muffle furnaces, including cleaning of the corresponding bricks for reuse.*
> *Filling in of heating flues and ducts with the rubble and waste resulting from dismantling the muffle furnaces.*
> *Installation of gas protection doors, window shutters, and windows,*
> *creation of wall openings and ducts needed for heating stoves, aeration and ventilation,*
> *plumbing and drainage work,*
> *re-arrangement of existing electrical wiring in accordance with floor plan,*
> *improvement of floors and partial installation of wooden floor,*
> *improvement of roof and painting of same with bitumen.*
> *2. Materials needed:*
> *500 kg of cement*
> *400 kg of bricks*
> *20 kg of steel rods*
> *50 m of railway rails*
> *24 pcs. timber, 4.80 m long, 10/15 cm*
> *10 pcs. timber, 3.90 m long, 10/15 cm*
> *102 sqm boards, 25 mm*
> *13 pcs. windows, one-sided, 60 x 80 cm*
> *2 pcs. doors, one-sided, 70 x 200 cm*
> *16 pcs. window shutters, gas-tight and shrapnel-proof*
> *7 pcs. doors, gas-tight and shrapnel-proof"*

On October 17, SS-*Sturmbannführer* Bischoff, head of the Construction Inspectorate of the Waffen-SS and Police Silesia, wrote a letter to the Central Construction Office regarding the start of the construction work, which, "due to urgency," could begin immediately without the usual bu-

---

[70] Letter from SS-*Sturmbannführer* Bischoff, Leiter der Bauinspektion der Waffen-SS und Polizei "Schlesien," to Zentralbauleitung of October 17, 1944. RGVA, 502-2-147, p. 124.
[71] RGVA, 502-1-401, p. 34. Cf. Document 14.

reaucratic formalities.[70] The work had already begun, though, because a document dated September 4 mentions "Construction of a gas-tight treatment room in the former crema. for the garrison physician," 5 percent of which had been completed.[72]

On November 2, 1944 Jothann drew up an "explanatory report for conversion of the old crematorium into an air-raid shelter for the SS infirmary with an operating room in CC Auschwitz O/S. BW 98M," in which he described the work to be done:[73]

> "*Conversion of the existing and available rooms of the old crematorium into an air-raid shelter for the SS infirmary with an operating room. The existing central walls and some partitions will be reinforced to 38 cm. Missing partitions will be built anew. An emergency operating room, two gas-locks, two flushing toilets[74] and a water faucet in the operating room are to be installed because a water supply line is available and the sewage line can be extended. Electric lighting will be installed. Heating will be by stoves.*"

Regarding the time schedule, Jothann adds:

> "*On account of its urgency, work has already started and will be completed within three weeks.*"

On the same day, Jothann also drew up a cost estimate[75] for a total amount of 4,300 RM, and a location sketch.[76] The work was completed in the second half of November.

---

[72] "*Aufstellung der im Bau befindlichen Bauwerke mit Fertigstellungsgrad*" (register of building works under construction with degree of completion), drawn up by SS-*Obersturmführer* Jothann on September 4, 1944. RGVA, 502-1-85, p. 2.

[73] RGVA, 502-2-147, p. 125.

[74] These toilets were initially planned as "*Trockenklosett*" (chemical toilets), see Document 5. The drainage pipes of these toilets can still be seen in the morgue today, see Document 35.

[75] "*Kostenüberschlag zum Ausbau des alten Krematoriums als Luftschutzbunker für SS-Revier mit einem Operationsraum im K.L. Auschwitz O/S. BW 98M*," RGVA, 502-2-147, pp. 126-126a.

[76] "*Lageskizze für den Ausbau eines Luftschutzbunkers für SS Revier*," RGVA, 502-2-147, p. 122.

Chapter 3:
The Witnesses

In this chapter, we will examine, in chronological order, the declarations of the main witnesses – former detainees and former members of the SS – who have spoken of homicidal gassings in the morgue of Crematorium I.

3.1. Stanisław Jankowski

On April 16, 1945, Stanisław Jankowski, who at that time chose to be called Alter Feinsilber,[77] made a deposition[78] in the course of the preparation of the trial of Höss, stating among other things that he had been assigned to work in Crematorium I in November 1942. This is what he had to say about the morgue:[79]

> "*This large hall had no windows, merely two traps in the ceiling and electric lights, as well as a door from the corridor[80] and a second one leading to the furnace room. This hall was called corpse hall [morgue]. It was used for storing corpses; at the same time, so-called 'rozwałka,' i.e., executions of detainees by shooting, took place there.*"

Hence, the morgue was not a gas chamber. In fact, he stated specifically:[81]

> "*I declare that at that time, i.e., in late 1942, there were not yet any gas chambers at Auschwitz. The only gassing action known to me from that period occurred in November or December 1942.*"

He was referring to the alleged gassing of the 390 members of the first "*Sonderkommando.*"[81] In her entry for that day, Danuta Czech states:[82]

> "*The 300 or so Jewish prisoners of the special unit assigned to digging up and incinerating the 107,000 bodies buried in mass graves are driven by the SS*"

---

[77] Another spelling of his family name was Fajnzylberg.
[78] Statement of Stanisław Jankowski (Alter Feinsilber), in: "Inmitten des grauenvollen Verbrechens. Handschriften von Mitgliedern des *Sonderkommandos*," *Hefte von Auschwitz*, special issue I, Verlag des Staatlichen Auschwitz-Birkenau Museums, 1972, p. 42.
[79] *Ibid.*, pp. 42f.
[80] Actually from the corpse washing room (*Waschraum*).
[81] *Ibid.*, p. 48.
[82] D. Czech, *Kalendarium der Ereignisse im Konzentrationslager Auschwitz-Birkenau 1939–1945*, Rowohlt Verlag, Reinbek 1989, p. 349.

from Birkenau to the Main Camp. There they are led into the gas chamber at Crematorium I and killed by gas. In this way the witnesses to the incineration of the bodies are eliminated."

Czech's sources are merely testimonies. They were given, moreover, after Jankowski made his statement. In fact, this alleged gassing lacks even the slightest documentary evidence, and the date of December 3, 1942 was simply invented by Czech on the basis of the above-mentioned declaration by Jankowski. Other than that, there is no document concerning this alleged "*Sonderkommando*" of 300 or 390 Jewish detainees. The only reference to it by Czech, dated July 4, 1942, is the following:[83]

"The so-called Sonderkommando, consisting of several dozen Jewish detainees, is being formed. They have to dig trenches near the Bunkers and bury the bodies of those killed in the gas chambers. This command is housed in one of the barracks in the men's camp at Birkenau. It is completely isolated from the other detainees."

The source used by Auschwitz Museum researcher Czech is the "Proceedings of the Delegatura of the Polish Government in Exile,"[83] *i.e.*, the documents published in the work "The Auschwitz Concentration Camp in the Light of the Proceedings of the Delegatura of the Polish Government in Exile" mentioned above.[4] It states, in fact, in the "Memorandum on the situation in the Country for the period of July 16 to August 25, 1942" that four detainees who had escaped from Auschwitz at the end of June 1942 had said the following, among other things:[84]

"From each group of new arrivals, several groups of ten very strong detainees were selected. They form a special company that dug the graves during the night and buried the dead. This totally isolated company was exterminated after a while in the gas chamber; its task was taken over by a fresh group."

Danuta Czech's reference to this text is therefore deliberately misleading, either because the report of the four escapees refers to a period prior to the end of June (hence the date of July 4 is wrong) or because at that time the "special company"[85] already existed.[86]

As far as the content of this report is concerned, we may ask how the four escapees had come to know that this unit would, after some time, be exterminated and replaced by another one, if the "*Sonderkommando*" of Birkenau mentioned by them was the first of its kind, which had not yet been exterminated at that time. Clearly, we are here at the very root of the

---

[83] *Ibid.*, p. 243.
[84] "Obóz koncentracyjny…," *op. cit.* (note 4), p. 37.
[85] At that time, the term "*Sonderkommando*" was still unknown.
[86] Danuta Czech's assertion is contradictory in itself: If the "*Sonderkommando*" assigned to the digging of mass graves for the allegedly gassed victims of the so-called "Bunkers" was established on July 4, 1942, who dug the mass graves for the victims allegedly gassed in "Bunker 1" between March 20 and July 3, 1942?

propaganda story about the periodic elimination of the "*Sonderkomman-dos.*"[87]

Danuta Czech is unable to furnish us with the name of even a single member of the first "*Sonderkommando*" of Birkenau, which was allegedly gassed in the morgue of Crematorium I. J.-C. Pressac, on the other hand, succeeded in finding one: Maurice Benroubi. This man claims to have been assigned to the "*Sonderkommando*" after his arrival at Auschwitz on July 23, 1942, and to have unceremoniously been transferred to the Jawischowitz camp on September 4, 1942.[88] Another self-styled member of the first "*Sonderkommando*," Dr. André Lettich, likewise survived the alleged gassing in Crematorium I, and in March 1943 was transferred (at his own request!) to the gypsy camp at Birkenau.[89]

In a report that is included in the so-called "Auschwitz Protocols," which started circulating in the spring of 1944, Alfred Wetzler writes:[90]

"On December 17, 1942, 200 young Jews from Slovakia who had been working in the so-called Sonderkommando at the gassing [operations] and the incineration of the corpses, were executed in Birkenau. The execution resulted due to a prepared mutiny and an attempt to escape, which had been revealed early on by a Jew. The unit was replaced by 200 Jews from Poland who had just arrived with a transport from Makow. Among those executed were: Alexander Weiss, Trnava; Fero Wagner, Trnava; Schneider Oskar, Trnava; Wetzler Dezider, Trnava; Aladar Spitzer, Trnava; Vojtech Weiss, Trnava."

At the Frankfurt Auschwitz trial, Alfred Wetzler returned to the question of the gassing of the "*Sonderkommando*":[91]

"One day in December 1942, the Birkenau Sonderkommando did not report for work. At the time it consisted of 300 men. Prior to that, I had received a letter from a detainee in this unit, in which he said good-bye to his sister who was likewise in the camp. On that day, many SS men were in the camp. Fifteen detainees were selected from the Sonderkommando. Together with Palitzsch and Stiwitz, Broad carried out this selection and took these 15 men to the morgue in Section B1b. It has remained unknown to me why exactly these 15 men were

---

[87] In the introduction to the book *Testimoni della catastrofe. Deposizioni di prigionieri del Sonderkommando ebraico di Auschwitz-Birkenau (1945)* (Ombre corte, Verona 2004, p. 16), Carlo Saletti wrote:
"Memoirs and critical texts on Auschwitz are legion, in which it is maintained that the life expectancy of the prisoners in the Sonderkommando did not exceed four months and that once that period was over, they were systematically eliminated. Neither of those two assertions is true."

[88] J.-C. Pressac, *op. cit.* (note 33), p. 162f.

[89] André Lettich, *Trente-quatre mois dans les Camps de Concentration. Témoignage sur les crimes "scientifiques" commis par les médecins allemands*, Imprimerie Union Coopérative, Tours 1946, pp. 27-30.

[90] APMO, *Akta obozowego RO*, tomo XXa, sygn. D-RO/129, pp. 22f.

[91] Hermann Langbein, *Der Auschwitz-Prozess. Eine Dokumentation*, Europa Verlag, Vienna 1965, pp. 531f.

chosen. The remaining 285 detainees from one of the shifts of the Sonderkommando had to report to the other side of the camp section. A larger number of SS men led this group to Auschwitz. The 15 that had been selected were shot by Palitzsch, Stiwitz, and Broad. At that time, there were mainly Jews from Slovakia in the Sonderkommando, with numbers in the 36,000s. They had come to Auschwitz from Lublin."

Alfred Wetzler was deported to Auschwitz from Slovakia on April 13, 1942, and registered as number 29,162. He therefore must have had direct knowledge about the men in the *"Sonderkommando"* who were allegedly gassed and whose names he had supplied. Before we check this detail, however, it is necessary to state that his declaration at the Auschwitz trial clashes violently with his report made in 1944: whereas in the latter the number of men in the *"Sonderkommando"* was 200 and the place of execution was Birkenau, during the trial the number had increased to 300 and the place of execution had moved to Auschwitz.

Wetzler is the only witness to give precise and verifiable information regarding the murder of the *"Sonderkommando,"* that is:
– the date: December 17, 1942
– the number of detainees: 200 (or 300)
– the nationality of the detainees: Slovakian Jews
– the origin of the detainees: Lublin concentration camp
– the ID numbers of the detainees: in the 36,000s

So let us check the data. A transport of Slovakian Jews did in fact arrive at Auschwitz from Lublin Concentration Camp on May 22, 1942: The 1,000 detainees that made it up received the ID numbers 36,132–37,131.[92] Obviously, we have here the transport Alfred Wetzler refers to and from which the 200 or 300 detainees of the *"Sonderkommando"* allegedly gassed on December 17, 1942 are said to have been selected.

Actually, due to the deplorable catastrophic hygienic and sanitary conditions in the Birkenau camp, 947 of these 1,000 detainees died between May 27 and August 15, 1942.[93] If, therefore, only 53 of these detainees were still alive on August 15, 1942, it is impossible for 200 or 300 of them to have been gassed on December 17, all the more so as 20 of these 53 detainees died between August 16, 1942 and March 1, 1943, as shown in Table 1 (next page).[94]

In fact, only one detainee from this transport died in December of 1942!

Furthermore, out of the six detainees Alfred Wetzler claims were murdered during the alleged elimination of the *"Sonderkommando"* on Decem-

---

[92] APMM, fot. 423, name list of the transport. The list also includes the dates of death of the detainees who died prior to August 15, 1942.

[93] AGK, NTN, **88**, p. 114, statistical data by Otto Wolken, and APMM, fot. 423.

[94] APMM, fot. 423, name list of the transport of May 22, 1942; Staatliches Museum Auschwitz-Birkenau (ed.), *Sterbebücher von Auschwitz*, K.G. Saur, Munich 1995.

Table 1: Entries in Auschwitz *Death Book* of Slovakian Jews from Lublin camp registered at Auschwitz on May 22, 1942, and confirmed dead between Aug. 16, 1942, and March 1, 1943.

ID no.	Last name	First name	Date of birth	Date of death	*Sterbebuch* no.
36179	Bauer	Ladislaus	Sept. 27, 1925	Aug. 16, 1942	21295
36650	Blau	Maximilian	Dec. 14, 1910	Aug. 16, 1942	22370
37045	Ehrenreich	Samuel	July 27, 1925	Aug. 16, 1942	21296
37056	Hoenig	David	Oct. 15, 1926	Aug. 16, 1942	21245
37098	Mozes	Imrich	Nov. 28, 1927	Aug. 16, 1942	21364
36829	Hajnal	Zoltan	Apr. 27, 1922	Aug. 22, 1942	23914
36767	Ringel	Heinz	July 28, 1921	Aug. 22, 1942	23863
37065	Klein	Ladislaus	Dec. 30, 1925	Aug. 24, 1942	24566
36492	Sachs	Leo	Feb. 4, 1900	Aug. 25, 1942	24900
36498	Gerler	Josef	Oct. 18, 1924	Sept. 4, 1942	27683
36900	Schlesinger	Aladar	Apr. 13, 1924	Sept. 12, 1942	30198
37039	Braunstein	Samuel	Nov. 18, 1926	Sept. 16, 1942	30894
36338	Mandel	Arnold	Mar. 18, 1912	Sept. 23, 1942	32464
36186	Joeger	Max	May 4, 1919	Oct. 6, 1942	34829
36774	Politzer	Wilhelm	May 27, 1913	Oct. 14, 1942	35883
36343	Engel	Vidor	May 3, 1907	Oct. 21, 1942	36947
37084	Adler	Isidor	July 24, 1924	Oct. 24, 1942	37330
37106	Fenster	Imrich	Aug. 11, 1926	Dec. 3, 1942	43046
36214	Rosenzweig	Josef	Feb. 7, 1915	Jan. 14, 1943	2116
37112	Margulies	Josef	Aug. 5, 1927	Mar. 1, 1943	12252

ber 17, 1942, only one appears in the Death Books: Dezider Wetzler, born at Trnava on March 11, 1908. He, however, died on July 10, 1942 (ID number 14676).

By 1947, the story of the gassing of the Birkenau "*Sonderkommando*" on December 17, 1942, had reached a certain degree of completion. On August 28, 1947, the former detainee Henryk Porębski made a deposition during the preparation of the Auschwitz garrison trial, in which he declared:[95]

> "*The first inmate unit of this kind was formed at Birkenau in April or May of 1942. It had 20 members. Up to June, this Sonderkommando was changed more or less every other week by killing the ones who belonged to it. From mid-1942 onward, it grew steadily, reaching 800 detainees in December 1942. On December 8, on the orders of Grabner, the whole unit was taken to the Main Camp at 9 in the morning, and was gassed in the gas chamber of the old crematorium. Some of the corpses were burnt in the crematorium, the others on pyres at Birkenau.*"

---

[95] AGK, NTN, 144, p. 127.

This account, again without any documentary evidence, was then used by the Krakow tribunal in its trial of Maximilian Grabner.[96] The alleged gassing of 200 or 300 or 800 detainees of the so-called "*Sonderkommando*" in the morgue of Crematorium I thus has no foundation in fact. This is confirmed by other documents.

Prior to their incineration, the detainees who died at Auschwitz were taken to a separate morgue, which was located in the basement of block 28, where their ID numbers were registered in a special register, the *Leichenhallenbuch* (morgue book). For December 3, 1942 – the "official" date set by D. Czech – this register shows the ID numbers of 125 deceased detainees; on the 4th, there are 118, and on the 5th, 102 such entries. From December 6 onward the number of deaths decreases significantly: 22 for the 6th, 48 for the 7th, 53 for the 8th. On the first two days of December, the numbers had been 86 and 59, respectively.[97] In November, there had been 1,688 deaths, 56 per day on average.[98] In December, the figure was 1,741, again an average of 56 deaths per day.[98]

Of the 125 detainees who died on December 3, fifteen were brought in from the Chełmek satellite camp, two from the Monowitz camp ("Buna"), and one from the Golleschau satellite camp.[99] Of the 118 dead inmates registered on December 4, nine had come from Monowitz.[100] Finally, of the 102 detainees who died on December 5, eleven came from Birkenau, two from the satellite unit at Budy, and six from Monowitz.[101] Hence, for the 345 detainees who died between December 3 and 5, 35 died outside the camp and only eleven at Birkenau; all other deaths occurred at the Auschwitz Main Camp.

Danuta Czech remains silent about the fact that the corpses of the detainees of the so-called *Sonderkommando* are not listed in the "*Leichenhallenbuch*." However, she claims that 64 registered detainees were killed by lethal injection on December 3, 78 on the 4th, and 60 on the 5th,[102] altogether 202 out of the total of 345.

The SS would have had no motive for not registering the members of the "*Sonderkommando*" allegedly gassed, and the fact that they do not appear in the registry at that time simply means that they were not killed. Besides, the gassed are said to have been incinerated in the crematorium, as stated by the witness Jankowski (see farther below). However, between

---

[96] GARF, 7021-108-39, p. 51a.
[97] AGK, OB, 385, *Leichenhallenbuch*, pp. 32-42.
[98] AGK, NTN, 143, *Leichenhallenbuch*. Analysis by J. Sehn, p. 142.
[99] AGK, OB, 385, *Leichenhallenbuch*, pp. 35f.
[100] *Ibid.*, pp. 37f.
[101] *Ibid.*, pp. 39f.
[102] D. Czech, *op. cit.* (note 82), pp. 349-352.

December 3 and 5, Crematorium I received 10 tons of coke,[103] sufficient for the incineration of (10,000 ÷ 28[104] =) 357 corpses. Hence, only the 345 corpses registered in the *"Leichenhallenbuch"* were cremated, and this demonstrates that the story of the gassing of the 300 or 390 or 800 members of the *"Sonderkommando"* is pure fiction.

That said, let us turn to Jankowski's testimony. He declared that he had heard from detainees employed in the crematorium that

> *"even before this gassing, some gassings had taken place in this same morgue and in other rooms of the crematorium."* (my emphasis).[105]

The alleged gassing "in other rooms of the crematorium" is absolute nonsense. Jankowski furthermore affirmed, and confirmed under oath on September 29, 1980, that, during the only homicidal gassing about which he could testify, he had been confined to the coke storage room together with other service personnel.[106]

He asserted, moreover, that the detainees of the crematorium *"Sonderkommando"* were assigned "for two days" to transporting the corpses of the 390 alleged gassed victims from the morgue to the furnace hall.[107] As there were nine[108] "ordinary workers" in the *"Sonderkommando"* who took 30 corpses of those who had been shot[109] to the furnace room every hour, it is clear that those two days were not needed for the transportation but for the incineration of the corpses. The three double-muffle furnaces of Crematorium I thus had a maximum capacity of (390 ÷ 2 =) 195 corpses per day, but this contradicts both the official account – 340 corpses per day – and Jankowski's own statement, according to which into each muffle

> *"could be placed up to 12 corpses, but in general one did not load more than 5, because this number burned more quickly,"*[110]

which is nonsense from the standpoint of heat technology.[111]

No less surprising is the fact that this witness, who claimed to have worked in Crematorium I from November 1941 until July 1943,[112] did not even know how the furnaces operated, because he asserted that "the corpses lay on grids *under which coke was burning."* (my italics)[110]

---

[103] APMO, D-AuI-4, Segregator 22, 22a, List of "Coke and coal for the crematoria in tons."
[104] As for the consumption of coke, cf. my study *The Cremation Furnaces of Auschwitz,"* *op. cit.* (note 38), p. 362.
[105] "Inmitten des grauenvollen Verbrechens," *op. cit.* (note 78), p. 48.
[106] J.-C. Pressac, *op. cit.* (note 33), p. 125.
[107] "Inmitten des grauenvollen Verbrechens," *op. cit.* (note 78), p. 49.
[108] *Ibid.*, pp. 43f.
[109] *Ibid.*, p. 45.
[110] *Ibid.*, p. 43.
[111] According to Jankowski, the cremation capacity of Crematorium I was 1,440 corpses per day. See farther below.
[112] "Inmitten des grauenvollen Verbrechens," *op. cit.* (note 78), pp. 42 and 52.

Actually, the coke burned in the gasifier, a vertical chamber lined with refractory bricks housed in a special brick structure, which was located *behind* the furnaces and which was connected to the individual muffles by a special opening through which the combustion gasses and flames passed from the gasifier into the associated muffle, where the corpse was placed on a grid.

On October 3, 1980, Jankowski stated the following under oath:[113]

"It is at Auschwitz that I saw for the first time a gassing in the morgue. This room had no windows, but there were ventilators in the ceiling. The two thick wooden doors of the room, one in the side wall, the other in the end wall, had been made gas-tight. The room was lit by electricity. The victims of this gassing were about 400 Jews brought from Birkenau. The men of the Sonderkommando, including myself, saw them enter the yard, then we were shut in the coke store. When the Sonderkommando men came out, they saw and I saw only their clothes in the yard. Thirty minutes later, the Sonderkommando was ordered to transport the corpses to the furnace, situated about five metres from the door of the morgue, in a separate room."

Between August 28 and September 6, 1985, Jankowski gave an account in Polish at the Auschwitz Museum under the name of Fajnzylberg, which was recorded by Franciszek Piper. On the subject of Crematorium I, he stated the following:[114]

"In the crematorium, the corpses of the detainees who died at the camp [and] *of those who had been murdered in the gas chamber were burned. I remember the gassing of some 400 members of the Sonderkommando who had been assigned to the open-air cremation of corpses or to other gassings.* […]

There were three furnaces in the crematorium; each one had 2 hearths. Into each opening one usually loaded 3 corpses. Only toward the end of work, 10–12 corpses would be loaded, which then burned in our absence. Such a load of corpses was not easy [to burn], *therefore the Kapos took care of it. The corpses were packed so tightly that a special stoking device was shoved underneath their arm.*[115] *The cremation of a load of 5 corpses took about half an hour.* [[116]…]

On the inside, the gas chamber was painted white; in the ceiling, as far as I remember, there were two openings for the introduction of the gas; there were no false showers, I do not remember any ventilators."

---

[113] J.-C. Pressac, *op. cit.* (note 33), pp. 124f.

[114] "Relacja" (Account) by Alter Fajnzylberg, August 28 to September 6, 1985. APMO, *Oświadczenia* (declarations), vol. 113, pp. 3f.

[115] The idea is that the corpses were loaded into the muffles by pushing them in with a special stoking device placed in the armpit.

[116] "*około pół godziny.*" For the 6 muffles of the crematorium, this corresponds to a cremation capacity of 1,440 corpses per day.

In this statement as well, we have a wealth of technical nonsense: a normal load was three corpses per muffle; five corpses would burn within half an hour; towards the end of the day one loaded 10–12 corpses. It is worthwhile noting here that one muffle of the Auschwitz crematorium furnaces could burn a single corpse in one hour.

It is, moreover, very curious to see that Jankowski did not know anything about "ventilators" in 1945, then miraculously remembered them in 1980, only to forget about them again in 1985!

3.2. Erwin Bartel

This Polish witness was interned at the Auschwitz camp between June 5, 1941 and October 26, 1944. After about three months, he was assigned to the Political Department of the camp, reporting to SS-*Unterscharführer* Hans Stark and SS-*Untersturmführer* Maximilian Grabner. On August 27, 1947, Bartel was questioned by Jan Sehn and declared the following about Grabner:[117]

> "*I personally saw him watching the murder of the victims with gas in the gas chamber of Crematorium I. He observed the development of the gassing from above before the Zyklon was thrown in.*"

Since the alleged gassings are said to have been carried out by the Political Department, to which the witness was assigned, his knowledge in this regard is somewhat vague.

At the end of the 1950s, at the time of the preparation of the Frankfurt Auschwitz trial, Bartel made a declaration in Poland, in which he described the alleged homicidal activity of Crematorium I in the following way:[118]

> "*In 1942 – in March or April as far as I can remember – arriving transports were gassed in the old crematorium next to the Main Camp. At that time, the large crematoria at Birkenau had not yet been built. Stark used to be very interested in these things and has taken part in them. Our windows looked out on the crematorium, and so I could see that Stark went there and returned from there. Stark was also responsible for the boxes with the toxic gas Cyklon B. At times, these boxes were kept in the corridor next to our offices.*"

This is a rather general statement and is moreover in disagreement with Danuta Czech's *Kalendarium*, according to which no transport said to have been gassed arrived in March or April 1942, and no homicidal activity went on during that time.[119] The Zyklon B, because of its dangerous nature, was kept at the SS infirmary under the responsibility of the SS garrison

---

[117] AGK, NTN, 135, p. 241.
[118] ZStL, ref. IV 402AR-Z 37/58, p. 619. The date of the declaration is not indicated.
[119] D. Czech, *op. cit.* (note 82), months indicated.

physician, and it is absolute nonsense that whole boxes of this dangerous disinfestant would have been kept – even if only "temporarily" – in a corridor outside of the offices of the Political Department under the responsibility of Grabner.

3.3. Filip Müller

Filip Müller was deported to Auschwitz from Slovakia on April 13, 1942 (the same transport as Alfred Wetzler's) and received the ID number 29236. He appeared as a witness of the prosecution at the 16th hearing of the trial of the Auschwitz camp garrison and made the following deposition, which has gone practically unnoticed until today and merits quoting in full:[120]

> "I was Auschwitz camp detainee No. 29236. I arrived at the Auschwitz concentration camp in April 1942. In May 1942 I was assigned to Block 11 and endured terrible sufferings. They consisted mainly in the fact that we could not have drinking water. On account of that, I had to go looking for leftover tea at 6 in the morning in the yard of Block 11, to 'organize' it, as this sort of activity was called in the camp.
>
> There, the Oberscharführer of Block 11 surprised me and took me to a special room. In the afternoon, the camp Kommandant Aumeier came to that room and, of course, asked me what I had done. Then he took me to another room, and after having brought in six more detainees, took us all to the gate of the Auschwitz camp. From the gate of the Auschwitz camp, the guards, ordered to do so by Aumeier, took us to the old crematorium of Auschwitz.
>
> In this way, I was present at the gassings in the crematorium from May 1942 until January 18, 1945. When Aumeier came to the crematorium, he signed us over to his subordinate Unterscharführer Stark who took us, with many beatings, to the gas chamber and opened it. In that chamber, there was the first Slovakian transport, gassed. These detainees had been gassed with their clothes on. As we were being beaten all the time and as we had no experience with the equipment, we caused a fire in the Auschwitz crematorium. For that reason, they could not burn the gassed victims.
>
> Upon Aumeier's initiative, at midnight that same day, two trucks were arranged, and the remaining corpses, some 800, were loaded on the trucks and taken to the vicinity of Birkenau. We arrived at Birkenau around 1 in the morning and were escorted by the Red Cross, which lit us from behind with its headlights. In that car was the accused Aumeier as well as the head of the Political Department, Grabner. Under violent blows and in a hurry we had to unload the corpses into trenches which still had water in them, thus, the work took two days.

---

[120] APMO, Proces załogi (Trial of the Auschwitz camp garrison), vol. VII, pp. 1-4.

After that, bloody and dirty as we were, they took us to Block 11 and locked us up in Cell 13. We were taken there by another Unterscharführer, who worked the night-shift, and the six of us were locked up. The next day, around 2 o'clock, after lunch, we were moved to the camp gate and waited there for the camp fire truck, painted green, in which were Aumeier and Grabner.

We climbed on the truck and went to the place where we had dumped the corpses the day before. First of all, we had to pile up the corpses in the mud in a heap, but as we could not do it properly, they beat the hell out of us. In all this, the persons giving the orders were the heads of the Political Department, Grabner and Aumeier. Then we spread chlorine over the corpses and were again locked up in Block 11, Cell 13.

We stayed in that cell for a year and a half, i.e., until the liquidation of the Auschwitz crematorium. I have known the defendants Aumeier and Grabner; I saw them at least once a day, practically until the liquidation of the Auschwitz crematorium, hence I want to mention a couple of events regarding their behavior.

At the time of the first massacre, the Kapos in the crematoria were German. One day, one of them had a bandaged hand. Unterscharführer Grabner approached him and asked: 'Fritz, why do you have a bandaged hand?' Fritz answered: 'I have killed another five Jews.' 'You stupid ass, that's not done with the hand, for this we have steel, and besides, if you kill five of them, there will be [another] *ten* [to kill]*, and if you kill ten, there will be* [another] *twenty.'*

In the Auschwitz camp, I also saw that the flesh of the non-Jewish detainees who were shot was used for various purposes. They were often shot in the presence of Mengele and others, whose names I do not know, and with Aumeier and Grabner present as well. Right away, the flesh of their calves would be put into boxes, and in this way they put aside 6 to 8 boxes of flesh each week.

It sometimes happened that a German delegation arrived with the swastika on the arm, asking in the presence of Aumeier and Grabner whether there was any human flesh. Aumeier used to say: 'We could also use horse meat, but that would be a waste!'

Unterscharführer Grabner was also guilty of sending out urns with the ashes of completely wrong victims, i.e., they filled 3000 urns with ordinary ash, which were then stored in the SS hospital in front of the crematorium, from where they would be sent out upon the orders of the Political Department.

I saw Aumeier and Grabner shooting Russian prisoners in Block 11 and Polish political prisoners, too. When Aumeier and Grabner felt that this [shooting] *was too slow, they used to beat them before they died and said faster*[sic]*.*

When the Polish political prisoners shouted 'Long live free Poland' before their execution, they took them aside and shot them in the stomach so that they would lie in agony for two or three hours.

Untersturmführer Grabner, as I have already said, was the main accomplice and promoter of the Auschwitz, not the Birkenau, crematorium.

There were cases in which corpses arrived from Kattowitz with their heads cut off; these corpses came from the Security Police at Kattowitz.

Grabner and Aumeier also took part in the selection of the sick and the weak in the hospitals and sent them to be shot. Untersturmführer Grabner participated in all the selections for the crematorium until 1943. All the selections which took place in the crematorium were done in the presence of Grabner until 1943, and also with Aumeier present. Normally, the shooting was done by Hauptscharführer Palit[z]sch and Unterscharführer Stark, who always received detailed instructions from them during the executions."

In a later declaration published by Ota Kraus and Erich Kulka, Müller speaks about these events in the following terms:[121]

"I arrived at Auschwitz on April 20, 1942, with the first Slovakian transport, and initially worked in this concentration camp like all the other detainees.

On May 24, 1942, one of my comrades and I suffered a great misfortune. We were very thirsty and were punished for water theft by being assigned to the gas chamber of the crematorium. The SS man led us there just when a few hundred corpses were lying there with their clothes still on and their baggage. We were unspeakably terrified when we realized what was ahead of us. Five detainees were already on the job; we had to get the corpses into the furnaces.

We were being supervised by the SS man Starck [Stark], who was about twenty years old. He hit me with his stick and advised me to get on with it, [or] I would eventually end up in the furnaces, too. Two Slovakian doctors, faced with this desperate situation, implored Stark to shoot them.

We had no experience with heating [the furnaces], and that had its consequences soon. Fire broke out in the crematorium, and it became impossible to burn the corpses. The SS accused us of sabotage, and four of our comrades were beaten to death because of this.

When the fire had been extinguished, seven new detainees were brought in. We loaded the remaining corpses on trucks, and then I went on the eeriest trip on my life.

It was late at night by then, and I sat on the last truck on a pile of corpses. Behind us there was a small car that showed on its sides and its roof a large red cross. The headlights of this car blinded us and shone upon us and our horrible load. Armed SS men were guarding us.

When the cars had reached the field behind the camp, they stopped by a swampy hole in the ground that had water in it, and we had to throw the corpses into this water. Around three in the morning we had finished this work and then returned to the camp. In the camp, they locked us up in a dark cell in the execution Block 11 and without food or water, bloody and dirty as we were, we had to wait there until noon the next day. When they let us out, each one of us was given a loaf of bread.

---

[121] O. Kraus, E. Kulka, *op. cit.* (note 27), pp. 130-132.

Then a fire truck took us to that hole; it was near Brzezinka, near the newly built concentration camp of Birkenau. We had to wait for a long time until the water had been scooped out of the hole. Not far away, we saw another group of detainees digging more holes; as we learnt later, this group was the Birke-nau Sonderkommando.[122]

And then it started. They herded us into the hole and we stood in the mud up to our belts. Our job was to lay the corpses in a heap and to make room for more. SS officers and men stood near the edge of the hole and enjoyed watching our horrible activity. They threw rocks at us to make us work faster.

When we had finally covered the corpses with chlorine and dirt, we went back into the camp, into our dark cell, in which we lived until August 1943. From morning till night we worked in the crematorium.

In the Crematorium I witnessed a great deal, scenes the world was never supposed to learn about.

They had not reckoned with my survival, the survival of an eyewitness, and even I myself had never thought that I would live to be free once again.

I cannot and I don't want to describe all these things in detail. It is way too much, and far too horrible for most people to believe. Not even I can comprehend today what I had to live through.

In the Auschwitz crematorium, I was forced to lend a hand to that infamous SS man, Palitzsch, who executed the sentences of the camp Gestapo. He murdered expertly and massively. The victims, usually political detainees, had to line up against the wall in groups of five, and Palitzsch shot them in cold blood.

It may have been June 17 or 18, 1942. On that fine sunny day everything was hastily cleaned, 'general cleaning' was the order of the day.

We watched the excited SS people and realized that something was going on, but we did not know what, we could only surmise that some visitor was expected.

Around ten o'clock, a high-ranking SS officer appeared in the door, wearing a white uniform, accompanied by two SS men – it was Himmler himself.

He inspected everything meticulously. He saw us in the room, in which the clothes and underclothes of those executed were stored.

When he saw those blood-stained clothes, he was surprised and asked our SS bosses why there was this blood.

Not satisfied with their answer, he became angry and said sharply: 'We need the clothes of these dirty dogs for our German people! It is a waste to gas those people with their clothes on!'

So after this visit, the gas chambers were converted into fake bathrooms with pipes and faucets, and the people had to undress before they were gassed.

In the summer of 1943 [1942], the furnaces and chimneys of the Auschwitz crematorium were gutted by a fire. The Nazi engineers rebuilt them, but three months later, everything collapsed all over again.

---

[122] As we have seen above, according to D. Czech this "*Sonderkommando*" was set up over two months later!

By that time, four crematoria were already in operation at Birkenau. We were moved there as well, as part of the Sonderkommando, into Block 13 of the men's main camp B IId.

The work in the Auschwitz crematorium also entailed filling the urns. We filled them with the ash and the dirt from the great pile and closed them with metal lids, on which we embossed the names of the victims, their date of birth and date of death, in accordance with the list we received from the Political Department. The urns were placed into boxes, some 20 x 20 x 40 cm, and labelled with the address of the family. They had to pay 2000 crowns for such an urn. No urns, however, were sent to the families of Jews.

Many such urns were sent to Bohemia, Moravia, and to other countries. But none of them contains the ashes of the person whose name is indicated on the urn.

When I was moved from Auschwitz to Birkenau, there was a store of some 4,000 already filled urns."

At the Auschwitz trial, Müller reformulated his account as follows:[123]

"Müller: I was brought to Auschwitz on April 13, 1942. The whole transport, some 250 men, Jews from Slovakia, was housed in Block 11. Once I was very thirsty and, together with a comrade, went into the yard of Block 11, where there was a cauldron full of tea. We wanted to drink. When we approached the cauldron, camp leader Aumeier and the block leader of [block] 11 came by and saw us. Aumeier said 'Just keep on drinking!' When we were near the vat, the SS men pressed our heads into the tea. I lost consciousness.

Later, I was told by the block elder to report to the block leader's office. A guard led me to the crematorium. I went into the yard. An Unterscharführer opened the gate. I recognized him, it was Stark. He beat me with a whip. Another door was opened, and I saw a furnace and three detainees who were working on a cart full of corpses. At the time, I was 20 years old and had never seen a corpse. I stopped. Stark beat us and yelled 'Get going, quick, quick, take the clothes off the corpses!'

There were perhaps 700 corpses there, with their clothes on, children, women, men, with packages strewn about. To the right of them, there were some 100 more people, with 'SU' on their clothes. Broken suitcases, bread, clothes were lying around, full of blood. We had to undress the corpses. Stark beat us all the time. It is a dreadful job to take clothes and shoes off rigid corpses. If we tore anything, Stark beat us again and again.

Presiding Judge: Did the corpses show any wounds?

Müller: Yes.

PJ: Had they been shot?

M: No, they had been gassed. I was to see that later. The corpses stood in front of the ventilators in the gas chamber, tightly packed. I saw a dead child hanging from the mother's breast. There were green crystals on the floor. There

[123] H. Langbein, *op. cit.* (note 91), pp. 459-463.

was a smell of almonds, or of hard spiritus. Even today, such a smell makes me sick.

There were seven of us in the Sonderkommando. At that time, two furnaces were in operation. In front of each furnace, there was a cart for the introduction of the corpses. Three corpses were loaded on the carts at one time. Those carts ran on rails. One day, three of us could not go on working. Stark drew his revolver and shot three comrades, Weiß, Goldschmidt, and Neumann, before my eyes.

Because the number of corpses increased rapidly, we had to load them on trucks and take them out to a field during the night. A large hole had been dug there, with water in it. There were four of us at the time, and we had to throw four to five hundred corpses into those holes. A car with a red cross stood near the hole and lit the scene with its headlights.

Afterwards, Stark led us back to Block 11. We came into a bunker cell without light. It was terrible to hear the clanking of the keys in the morning. We were given soup. Three new detainees, Frenchmen, were brought into the cell. Then we were all taken to the motor pool again and taken to the hole in a fire truck. The car pumped the water out of the hole, and we had to climb into the ditch, which was now very swampy, and lay the corpses on a pile. Near the pit, Grabner, Aumeier and others from the SS were standing. Stark was in charge of the operation. We could hardly remove the corpses; they fell apart in our hands. Arms tore off. The corpses were full of water. But Stark treated us like animals.

Two French comrades could not continue. Stark yelled 'What's the matter with you Moritzes!,' took out his pistol, and shot the two who had been leaning on the dead. Finally, we had to return to the camp on the double. We were covered with blood and dirt. They took us as we were to the bunker, Cell 13 this time. There was light in it. It was a dreadful night. We had collapsed, mentally and physically. We slept on the floor, like animals.

When the block leader brought us the food the next day, we asked to be allowed to wash ourselves. He let us go up into the washing room, and we were given other clothes, too, and were then taken back into Cell 13. At nightfall, we heard shouts in the yard 'Fishing command, get ready!'

I can imitate Stark's way of shouting even today. It meant that we now had to put on our wooden clogs. We were taken into the yard and into the crematorium. Two Slovak detainees came along this time. Stark took us to the crematorium, lined us up against the wall, and told us to wait for further orders. We were not to speak to anyone, otherwise we would be shot.

After some time, the doors of the yard were opened, and some 350 Jewish women, men and children were brought in. Grabner, Aumeier, Stark, and others from the SS were present. Stark yelled, 'Now, everyone undress!' Later, I saw from the clothes that they were Polish Jews. They must have known that something was not right and undressed only slowly. Stark and the others kept on yelling 'Get on with it, take your clothes off!' Stark beat the people with a whip.

I saw a man who wanted to take his tie off – but he did not have one on. The children went to their parents, but they did not cry. They were probably Jews from the ghetto. Then they were all led into the gas chamber. There was only one ventilator there, and the lights were on. The door was closed, and Stark ordered, 'Pick up those rags!'

Again, the gate was opened and again, 300 people entered. It was the same thing once again. After the gas had been fed into the chamber from the roof of the crematorium, there was heavy coughing, children and adults screamed, there was chaos. After a while, things quieted down, the coughing subsided, and we saw Stark coming down from the roof with his gas mask.

We were ordered to search the clothes and to put all valuables, dollars, gold, and other things into a box. Stark stood near the box and pocketed what he liked.

At that time, May and June 1942, gassings took place either before the morning roll call or after the evening roll call, never during the day. […] I watched Stark at his job for something like six weeks. During this time, he must have taken at least ten or eleven thousand people into the gas chambers."

Finally, as I have already mentioned, in 1979 Müller published a book of memoirs, in which he again described events in the Auschwitz crematorium.

Before we examine the declarations of this witness in detail, it must be emphasized that in his deposition during the trial of the Auschwitz camp garrison he did not mention at all his activity as a member of the so-called "*Sonderkommando*" in the crematoria at Birkenau. He did mention this in the declaration published by Kraus and Kulka, but devoted less than 45 percent of his story to it, a story, which, in any case, is made up of fanciful anecdotes, such as the removal of human flesh from executed detainees for culturing bacteria (although this no longer took place at Auschwitz, but in Crematorium V of Birkenau), or the systematic draining of the blood of young women (for German military hospitals) or the account about SS-*Hauptscharführer* Moll, who had the habit of throwing Jewish babies "into the boiling human fat"![124] The same historical value can be assigned to the little tale of the Kapo who regularly killed Jewish detainees and was reprimanded by the SS only because he had hurt his hand in doing so.

In his 1979 book of memoirs, Müller devoted 25 percent of the text to events in Crematorium I and the remaining 75 percent to happenings in the Birkenau crematoria: from 0 to 75 percent, a most astounding literary progression!

---

[124] O. Kraus, E. Kulka, *op. cit.* (note 27), pp. 133f.

The witness is not even certain of the date of his arrival at Auschwitz, for he gives it either as April 13 or April 20, 1942. His ID number (29236) was assigned on April 13, the day on which a transport of Slovak Jews arrived at the camp, which, however, comprised 1077 Jews, 634 men and 443 women,[125] and not 250, as the witness declared.

The events surrounding his assignment to the crematorium are anything but clear. Being thirsty, he – by himself and simultaneously together with another detainee – goes out looking for "leftover tea" which, however was "a cauldron full of tea" or "the vats with tea for the night,"[126] hence not really leftovers.

Strangely, however, he was punished and sent to the crematorium for "theft of water." He was apprehended by the *Blockführer* of Block 11 and by Aumeier, who told him sarcastically to go on drinking, but at the same time came to Müller's cell in the afternoon to ask him why he was there, because he did not know.

The witness was sent to the crematorium together with six other detainees, hence altogether seven. But after the first day at work they "locked up the six of us" in Block 11, even though no one had been lost. Or else Müller was taken, together with his comrade who was (or was not) present when they stole the tea, to the crematorium where there already were five detainees at work, so that together they would again be seven. Of those, however, four were killed the same day, having been made responsible for the fire that had broken out in the crematorium. Once the fire was under control, another seven detainees were assigned to the crematorium. Hence, before they started out on the work of burying the corpses, there were now ten detainees.

According to another version of the story, there were seven detainees in the "*Sonderkommando*," three of whom were shot, so that there were only four of them left when the burying started. In Müller's book, finally, there are three[127] detainees who were shot for sabotage, and those employed in the burials the first night are said to have been seven.[128]

The corpses to be buried were loaded on one truck,[127] or two, or three. The detainees doing this job during the first night were, as we have just seen, four, seven, or ten. The corpses – alternatively "some 800" and 400 to 500 – were thrown into one or several pits. Here the ground water was pumped out by a "fire truck" and, at the same time, by a "motor pump."[129]

Let us now move on to a review of what the witness has to say about the crematorium and the "gas chambers."

---

[125] D. Czech, *op. cit.* (note 82), p. 197.
[126] F. Müller, *op. cit.* (note 32), p. 19.
[127] *Ibid.*, p. 33.
[128] *Ibid.*, p. 37.
[129] *Ibid.*, p. 40.

On May 24, 1942, Müller was assigned to work in the camp crematorium. He noted right away the round chimney of this building,[130] which, however, was square.[131] Then he was led into the morgue where, among suitcases and backpacks, there were dead men and women who still had their clothes on. The witness was given the order to undress them.

Apparently, the SS, after eight months of alleged homicidal gassings, had not yet understood that it was easier to have the victims undress before they were gassed! According to the witness Walter Petzold, this "disastrous mistake" had been committed by the SS only on the occasion of the first nebulous homicidal gassing in Bunker 11.[132] They thus had learned their lesson at that time. The claim by the witness that the undressing of the corpses of the allegedly gassed victims was begun because of an order from Himmler is therefore ludicrous.

As far as that visit is concerned, it is an established fact that it took place on July 17 and 18, 1942, and Himmler could not have inspected the crematorium "around ten o'clock," because he was received at Kattowitz by *Gauleiter* Bracht, SS-*Obergruppenführer* Schmauser and by Höss at 3:15 p.m.; from Kattowitz he was accompanied to the camp, which he inspected even later.[133] There is no proof that Himmler ever inspected the crematorium. The photographs taken during the visit show Himmler wearing a gray uniform,[134] and Müller thus could not have seen him wearing "a white uniform."

The alleged disguise of the morgue as a "wash-rooms with pipes and faucets" is in contradiction to Jankowski's declaration, mentioned above, according to which there were "no false showers" in the alleged gas chamber. Hans Stark expresses himself in similar terms (see Section 3.8).

Müller did not overlook the "little greenish-blue crystals" or simply "green" crystals spread out on the floor of the morgue,[135] the residue of Zyklon B, which, however, did not consists of "greenish-blue crystals" but of gypsum granules, white in color. On account of its dangerous nature, the residue would be removed from the disinfestation chambers as soon as the test for toxic substances (*Gasrestprobe*) yielded negative results and thus

---

[130] *Ibid.*, pp. 22 and 31.

[131] "Inventory plan of building No. 47a, BW 11. Crematorium" (*Bestandplan des Gebäudes Nr. 47a. B.W. 11. Krematorium*) of April 10, 1942. Cf. Document 4.

[132] W. Petzold, "Bericht über die erste Vergasung von Gefangenen in deutschen Konzentrationslagern, Mauthausen den 17. Mai 1945." Staatsanwaltschaft beim LG Frankfurt (Main), Strafsache beim Schwurgericht Frankfurt (Main) gegen Baer und Andere wegen Mordes (investigation files to the Frankfurt Auschwitz trial), ref. Js 444/59, Vol. 31, p. 5312.

[133] Cf. in this respect my study *Special Treatment in Auschwitz. Origin and Meaning of a Term*, 3rd ed., Castle Hill Publishers, Uckfield 2016, pp. 16-25 and 118.

[134] AGK, NTN, 97, pp. 21-31, photographs of Himmler's visit.

[135] F. Müller, *op. cit.* (note 32), p. 24.

allowed the specialists to enter the room wearing their gas masks.[136] This would also have been true for any homicidal gassings, and therefore the witness cannot have seen Zyklon B residues in the alleged homicidal gas chamber. In fact, he has given a false description.

To his great surprise, Müller finds in the "gas chamber" the corpse of a girl with whom he had gone to school, and therefore the transport came from Slovakia. Indeed, the "gas chamber" held "the first Slovakian transport to be gassed," as he declared during the trial of the Auschwitz camp garrison.

Actually, according to Danuta Czech's *Kalendarium*, on May 24, 1942, there was no homicidal gassing, let alone of a Jewish transport from Slovakia. After April 29, in fact, the next Jewish transport from Slovakia arrived at Auschwitz on June 20, 1942, and the 659 persons that made it up were all duly registered! Hence Müller's account of the first homicidal gassing is a complete invention.

Then *Unterscharführer* Stark allegedly ordered the corpses to be burnt:[137]

> "Stark gave orders to switch on the ventilators. A button was pushed and they began to rotate. Soon, however, they were turned off again, once Stark had looked into the furnaces and convinced himself that the fire was burning well."

This sentence, which refers to the pre-heating phase of the furnaces, is nonsense. Each one of the 3 double-muffle furnaces was equipped with a blower driven by a three-phase electric motor of 1.5 HP and of the corresponding ductwork, which entered into the rear part of the furnace and ran through the brickwork above the two muffles. Two more pipes branched out from it in the upper part of the two muffles and fed into the latter by means of four openings in the muffle roof. The function of the blowers, therefore, was not to fan the fire of the gasifiers, but to feed combustion oxygen into the muffles. In the pre-heating phase of the furnaces, this would only have resulted in cooling the refractory lining of the muffles.

Müller goes on to accurately describe the device for introducing the corpses into the furnaces, but forgets an essential element, the pair of rollers attached to a fold-away frame, which was secured by a suitable supporting bar welded to the anchors of the furnace in front of the muffles. The omission probably stems from the fact that on the two furnaces poorly rebuilt by the Poles in the years after the war, the rollers had not been installed, whereas the device for introducing the corpses was otherwise correctly mounted.

---

[136] Cf. in this respect my article "Auschwitz: 'Gas Testers' and Gas Residue Test Kits," in: *The Revisionist*, 2(2) (May 2004), pp. 150-155.
[137] F. Müller, *op. cit.* (note 32), pp. 25f.

How many furnaces were in operation? At the Auschwitz trial, the witness declared: "at that time, two furnaces were in operation," but in his book he writes "all six furnaces were burning."[138] After the pre-heating period, the corpses were introduced into the furnaces – three at a time.[139] About this the witness states:[140]

"For the cremation of three corpses, the big wheels had estimated 20 minutes, and it was up to Stark to make sure that this would be accomplished"

He then adds that in one hour 54 corpses could be burnt in the three double-muffle furnaces, *i.e.*, three corpses every twenty minutes in each muffle. We are here in the realm of technological fantasy. The cremation capacity of the Auschwitz furnaces was one corpse per muffle per hour, a total of six corpses per hour in the six muffles. The witness has multiplied the capacity of the furnaces by a factor of nine!

Müller then relates that the crematorium personnel had forgotten "to shut down the ventilators of one furnace"[141] – which is wrong because each furnace had only one ventilator – with the following result:[141]

"The flames had been fanned so strongly and the fire had already reached an intensity such that the refractory bricks in the chimney came loose and the furnace burnt through, with the bricks falling into the flue that linked the furnace to the chimney."

This is another nonsensical statement. As has been explained above, the function of the blower was not to fan the fire, but to feed combustion air into the muffle. Because the blower brought in cold air, if air had been fed in, the result would have been the exact opposite of what the witness' version: the two muffles of the furnace would have cooled to the point of extinguishing the gasifier for lack of draft.

The "Instructions for the operation of the coke-fired Topf double-muffle cremation furnace" specifies, in fact, for such a case:[142]

"This temperature rise can be countered by blowing in air."

Furthermore, no furnace caught fire or was otherwise damaged in May–June 1942. Hence, Müller's story is historically false as well. In that period, only one such incident was recorded, which, however, did not involve the furnaces. On May 13, the head of the camp administration requested the Central Construction Office to "repair the chimney and the engine house[143] of the crematorium."[144] The work was done on May, 14 and 15.

---

[138] *Ibid.*, p. 25.
[139] *Ibid.*, p. 27.
[140] *Ibid.*, p. 29.
[141] *Ibid.*, p. 31.
[142] APMO, BW 11/1, p. 3.
[143] The little shed next to the crematorium and the chimney which housed the motor of the forced draft system.

The first item did, in fact, not concern the chimney as such, but the "chimney flue" which linked the three furnaces to the chimney: 50 refractory bricks were replaced and 50 kg of refractory mortar were used.[145]

On May 30, SS-*Oberscharführer* Josef Pollock informed Bischoff that the chimney's steel bands had loosened and cracks had appeared in the brickwork.[146] This led to the decision, as we shall see later, to knock down old chimney and rebuilt it, but all this lends no support whatsoever to the fairy-tale of the fire invented by our witness.

Hence, the witness has lied not only about the gassing of the Slovakian transport, but also about the fire in the crematorium.

This enigmatic fire – Müller continues – also spread to the furnace hall, and was brought under control only in the evening: the crematorium had become inoperable.[147] It went back into service after a few days,[148] *i.e.*, toward the end of May, when a transport of Jews arrived from Sosnowitz.[149] On that occasion, 600 persons are said to have been gassed in the morgue of the crematorium, if we follow Müller.[150]

However, according to the Auschwitz *Kalendarium*, the first transport of Jews from Sosnowitz arriving after May 30, 1942 (the day of Müller's assignment to the crematorium) came to Auschwitz on June 17 and was allegedly gassed, in its entirety, in "Bunker 1" of Birkenau![151]

After three days of inactivity, if we follow Müller, another transport of a few hundred persons was likewise gassed in the morgue.[152] On this occasion, we encounter for the first time the alleged deceptive speech designed to calm the victims.[153] This allegedly took place at the end of May 1942, because the witness declares:[154]

> *"In this way, from the end of May onwards, one transport after another disappeared in the Auschwitz crematorium."*

---

[144] *"Verwaltung KL Auschwitz. Bestellschein Nr. 451"* of May 13, 1942. APMO, BW11/5, p. 3: *"Den Kamin und das Motorenhaus des Krematoriums instandzusetzen"* (to repair the chimney and the motor shed of the crematorium).
[145] *"Aufstellung der ausgeführten Bauarbeiten."* May 20, 1942. APMO, BW 11/5, pp. 5f., and *"Bericht über ausgeführte Arbeiten im Krematorium"* of June 1, 1942. APMO, BW11/5, pp. 1f.
[146] RGVA, 502-1-314, p. 12 and 502-1-312, p. 64.
[147] F. Müller, *op. cit.* (note 32), p. 32.
[148] *Ibid.*, p. 49.
[149] *Ibid.*, p. 53.
[150] *Ibid.*, p. 54.
[151] D. Czech, *op. cit.* (note 82), p. 230.
[152] F. Müller, *op. cit.* (note 32), pp. 57-62.
[153] *Ibid.*, p. 61.
[154] *Ibid.*, p. 63.

Therefore, all of this – the three gassings and the fire – happened between May 24 and 31. However, according to Czech's *Kalendarium*,[155] no Jewish transport arrived at Auschwitz during that time.

The witness goes on to state that during this period the damage to the crematorium also occurred which required the rebuilding of the chimney. Here, Müller says:[156]

> "*In place of the round chimney that had been destroyed during the fire at the crematorium, the bricklayer unit erected an enormous new quadrangular chimney.*"

Then he adds:[157]

> "*The continuous operation, especially the strain on the furnaces that went with it and that originally had not been taken into account, apparently caused the refractory bricks of the inner lining to disintegrate, threatening the collapse of the chimney. For that reason, in the summer of 1942 a new quadrangular chimney with a double lining of refractory was attached to the furnaces. During this period, however, the operation of the furnaces was not discontinued. The unit working on the chimney was about 30 heads strong. These were mainly Jewish detainees.*"

Hence the witness either attributes two different causes to the damaging of the same chimney or else refers to two different chimneys. The first hypothesis entails an obvious contradiction, the second one is factually incorrect.

Actually, as has been noted above, the chimney of Crematorium I showed initial damage at the end of May 1942, but had not been "destroyed." When dangerous cracks appeared in the brickwork, it was decided to knock it down and build a new one. The new chimney was put up by 688 detainees (and not by "about 30") between July 12 and August 8, the old one was demolished on July 6.

Filip Müller's claim that the crematorium remained in operation during this period of construction is obvious nonsense, because it was necessary to build new flues, one 12.20 m long linking furnaces 1 and 2 to the new chimney, the other 7.375 m long for furnace 3.[158] In July, coke deliveries to the crematorium were drastically reduced: after a shipment of 5 tons on July 18, the next shipment arrived only on August 10,[159] which means that the crematorium certainly remained inactive for some 20 days, July 20 through August 9.

---

[155] D. Czech, *op. cit.* (note 82), pp. 216-218.
[156] F. Müller, *op. cit.* (note 32), p. 65.
[157] *Ibid.*, p. 74.
[158] Robert Koehler, "*Rauchkanal für die Zentral-Bauleitung der Waffen-SS und Polizei Auschwitz O.S.*" of August 11, 1942. RGVA, 502-2-23, p. 18.
[159] APMO, D-AuI-4, Segregator 22, 22a, List of "Coke and coal for the crematoria in tons," p. 2.

Filip Müller returns to the question of the chimney, writing:[160]

"The SS Construction Office[161] had placed great hopes for a smooth operation of the crematorium in the new quadrangular chimney. Soon, however, it turned out that it was not up to its task. During operation, refractory bricks continually fell off, blocking the flue through which the smoke had to pass. Jewish transports, still arriving as before, could no longer be 'handled' in the crematorium without a hitch. For that reason, the operation had to be curtailed in the fall of 1942."

Actually, the crematorium was put back into operation at full capacity without the new chimney having been properly dried: The brick-work, still humid, was damaged by the evaporation of water it contained, causing new cracks. On August 13, Bischoff, referring to a discussion he had had with SS-*Hauptsturmführer* Mulka the day before, sent the following letter to the camp command:[162]

"On the basis of the telephone conversation mentioned above, the camp command was informed that because of being heated too soon (all 3 furnaces are in operation), damage to the brick-work of the new chimney unit has already appeared. Since the 3 cremation furnaces were put into operation before the chimney's brick-work mortar could completely harden, any further responsibility [on the part of this officer] for this unit must be refused."

The witness does not explicitly say when the alleged gassings in Crematorium I were stopped, but he, too, speaks of the nebulous gassing of the men from the so-called "*Sonderkommando*," which is said to have occurred "in mid-December 1942."[163] If we follow Jankowski, this should have been the last gassing.

Müller assigns a sizeable number of victims to the alleged gas chamber of Crematorium I:[164]

"Tens of thousands of Jews from Upper Silesia, Slovakia, France, Holland, Yugoslavia, from the ghettos of Theresienstadt, Ciechanów, and Grodno were killed and cremated here."

In the deposition he made during the Auschwitz trial, mentioned above, he was even more precise:

"At that time, roughly in May and June 1942, gassings took place either before the morning roll call or after the evening roll call, never during the day. […] I watched Stark at this job for something like 6 weeks. During this time, he drove at least ten or eleven thousand people into the gas chambers."

---

[160] F. Müller, *op. cit.* (note 32), p. 79.
[161] Recte: SS Central Construction Office.
[162] RGVA, 502-1-312, p. 27.
[163] F. Müller, *op. cit.* (note 32), p. 80. F. Müller mentions neither the precise date nor the number of those allegedly gassed.
[164] *Ibid.*, p. 83.

Müller was assigned to the crematorium on May 24, 1942. The crematorium was shut down between July 19 or 20 and August 9 because of the demolition of the old chimney and the construction of the new one. In the autumn of that year, the crematorium was moreover used only in a limited way. Therefore, these "tens of thousands" of victims must have been killed between the end of May and the middle of July as well as in September of 1942.

However, according to Czech's *Kalendarium*, no homicidal gassing took place during the latter half of May, and in June the approximately 7,000[165] Jews allegedly killed are said to have been gassed in the so-called Bunker 1.[166] For July and September, Czech indicates no location for the alleged gassings,[167] but uses only the standard phrase "the [...] remaining deportees are killed in the gas chambers," with the "gas chambers" referring to "Bunkers" 1 and 2.

Müller claims that the alleged gas chamber of Crematorium I had served "from the very beginning only as a reserve installation for the two extermination facilities set up at Birkenau,"[160] *i.e.*, for the so-called "Bunkers." However, from the standpoint of orthodox historiography, the "Bunkers" did not need to make use of any reserve capacity, because the highest average daily rate of those claimed to have been gassed – for the month of August – was less than 1,200 per day in the two "Bunkers," whereas Czech's *Kalendarium* lists 2,000 people as having been gassed on two occasions – on June 17 and 20, 1942 – "in Bunker No. 1"[168] alone. Therefore, both "Bunkers" together would have had a gassing capacity of at least 4,000 persons per day, more than three times the average maximum daily load indicated above. What is more, out of the 7,000 allegedly gassed victims mentioned above, 6,000 belonged to transports for which there exists no document and which, pending proof of the contrary, have to be considered fictitious.[169]

In addition, the assertion that "tens of thousands of Jews [...] were killed and cremated" in the crematorium is refuted categorically by the amount of coke supplied to the crematorium. Between June and December 1942 it received 200.5 tons of coke,[170] sufficient for the cremation of a the-

---

[165] This figure includes an alleged transport of Jews from Ilkenau of unknown size, said to have been gassed in its entirety. I have given it the size of two other, similar transports, but which allegedly arrived from Sosnowitz: 2,000 persons.

[166] D. Czech, *op. cit.* (note 82), pp. 213-239.

[167] The only exception is the transport of Jews from Slovakia on July 4, for which D. Czech mentions the gassing of 628 persons "in the Bunkers." D. Czech, *op. cit.* (note 82), p. 243.

[168] D. Czech, *op. cit.* (note 82), pp. 230 and 232.

[169] C. Mattogno, *op. cit.* (note 133), pp. 35f.

[170] APMO, D-AuI-4, Segregator 22, 22a, List of "Coke and coal for the crematoria in tons," pp. 2f.

oretical maximum number of (200.5÷28=) 7,160 corpses.[104] Filip Müller eventually admits that in the crematorium "also the dead were cremated who had died in other camp areas,"[171] *i.e.*, those who had died a "natural" death. Thus it is clear that those 200.5 tons of coke must have been sufficient to burn both the dead from the camp – those registered in the *"Leichenhallenbuch"* – *and* those allegedly gassed. But the corpses documented come first. For the period of June through December 1942, the *"Leichenhallenbuch"* lists 9,399 persons deceased,[172] which means that the amount of coke supplied to the crematorium was not even sufficient to burn all the corpses stemming from the camp.[173] It is thus impossible that "tens of thousands" of Jews were "killed *and cremated*" in Crematorium I, as the witness maintains.

With respect to the alleged gas chamber, the witness claims that it possessed "six camouflaged openings" for the introduction of Zyklon B[174] and "a big ventilator"[135] installed "on the ceiling", which was somehow damaged by the alleged fire in the furnace hall.[147] But in his deposition at the Auschwitz trial, Müller declared: "The corpses stood in front of the ventilators in the gas chamber, tightly packed," then, contradicting himself, he added: "There was only one *ventilator*, the lights were on." But if the ventilator(s) was (or were) installed in the ceiling, how could people stand "in front" of them?

In conclusion, we may say that Müller has woven into a web of actual facts a dense tissue of fibs, which he has presented in a different way each time he recounts them. His initial transgression was obviously the literary pretext of justifying his being sent to the crematorium as "punishment." Then, too, his blatant lies about the gassing of the Slovakian transport and the fire in the crematorium are literary pretexts for introducing the story of the burials, again as a "punishment."

It is no accident that during the Auschwitz trial, fearing that he would be exposed, he gave up this lie and invented an entirely different story: the corpses were taken to the hole (or to the holes) no longer on account of the nebulous fire ("now the crematorium was, of course, no longer operational"[147]), but "because the number of corpses increased rapidly," *i.e.*, because the capacity of the furnaces was insufficient.

Because at this trial Müller made his depositions under oath, he either told the truth on this occasion, and thus obviously lied in his other declarations, or else he told the truth in his other declarations, and thus committed

---

[171] F. Müller, *op. cit.* (note 32), p. 72.
[172] AGK, NTN, 143, *Leichenhallenbuch*. Analysis by J. Sehn, p. 142.
[173] The corpses left over were buried and later incinerated in the open air at Birkenau.
[174] F. Müller, *op. cit.* (note 32), p. 62.

perjury at the Auschwitz trial (or both declarations are lies). Whichever way you look at him, he remains a liar.

The Frankfurt tribunal did not take Müller's account very seriously and declared of it:[175]

> "*The presentation of the witness Müller about the gassing of the Slovakian Jews is not very clear. Moreover, the court knows that at that time gassings no longer took place in the small crematorium, but in the farmhouses that had been adapted for the purpose.*"

Summarizing, S. Jankowski and F. Müller, the only – self-styled – survivors of the "*Sonderkommando*" of Crematorium I, have made declarations that are not only historically false and technically nonsensical, but are also mutually contradictory. In particular, one of them affirms that the alleged gas chamber had six openings and one ventilator, the other that it had two openings and no ventilator (or contradictorily states that it had "ventilators").

3.4. Hans Aumeier

SS-*Hauptsturmführer* Hans Aumeier held the post of "*1. Schutzhaft-lagerführer*" (first leader of the protective custody camp) of the Auschwitz camp from February 16, 1942, until August 15, 1943. In October 1943 he was made commandant of Vaivara concentration camp in Estonia, and from February 1945 onwards he was in charge of Mysen concentration camp in Norway; in that country he was arrested by the British on June 11, 1945.

In a report written on July 25, 1945, he stated:[176]

> "*As far as I remember, it was in November or December 1942 that the first gassing of about 50–80 Jewish detainees was undertaken. This took place in the morgue of the crematorium in Camp I, under the direction of the garrison physician, of Untersturmführer Grabener [Grabner], of the L.K.[177] and a number of medics. I was not present at the time and did not know beforehand that this gassing would take place, either. Towards me, the L.K. was always very distrustful and taciturn. It was only the next day that the garrison physician, Grabner, Ustfhr [Untersturmführer] Hessler [Hössler], Hptsfhr [Haupt-scharführer] Schwarz and I were called to the L.K., who informed us that the order of the RFSS has come from RSHA-Berlin that all Jewish detainees unfit for work as well as the sick judged by the doctor as not being fit for work in the future are to be gassed in order to avoid the spread of epidemics. He stated*

---

[175] H. Langbein, *op. cit.* (note 91), *op. cit.*, p. 884.
[176] PRO, File WO.208/4661. Report by H. Aumeier of July 25, 1945, pp. 5f.
[177] L.K., *Lagerkommandant*, commandant of the camp.

further that the first detainees had been gassed the previous night, but that the crematorium had turned out to be too small and could not cope with the cremations, so that in the crematorium[178] now under construction at Birkenau, gas chambers were being included. […]
In the period that followed, some 3 or 4 gassings were still carried out in the old crematorium. This always took place in the evening hours. There were 2–3 air shafts in the morgue, and 1–2 medics wearing gas masks poured bluegas through them. We ourselves were not allowed to get close, and the Bunker was opened only the following day. As the doctor said, the people had died within 1/2 to 1 M. [minute]."

As I have documented in a separate study,[179] Aumeier thought initial that he should be frank about Auschwitz, but eventually realized that he had to adopt the "truth" of his British interrogators, exactly as happened with Höss. This propagandistic "truth" was shaped to fit the declarations of self-styled eyewitnesses, in particular those interrogated by the English during the preparation of the Belsen trial and those interrogated by the Poles for the Höss trial.

As far as Aumeier's above declaration is concerned, we must first of all underline the curious coincidence of the date of the first alleged gassing in Crematorium I ("in the month of November or December 1942") with the date given by Jankowski ("in November or December 1942"). As that dating is wrong according to orthodox historiography, the coincidence is unlikely to be an accident.

The alleged Himmler order, which was issued inexplicably late, is also quite mysterious, as he could certainly have ordered detainees unfit for work to be killed, but why would he have ordered them to be gassed at a point when there were as yet no gas chambers at Auschwitz? And gas them with what? With the "bluegas" (*Blaugas*)? Actually, this was not hydrogen cyanide, but simply "fuel gas, a lighting gas, named after its inventor, [a man by the name of] Blau."[180] This "bluegas" was poured into the alleged gas chamber not through appropriate openings but through "air shafts." (How can one pour gas anyway?) The number of these air shafts (2–3: but were there 2 or were there 3?) copies, with some wavering, the number given by Jankowski (2 openings).

On the other hand, if the number of those allegedly gassed was hardly "about 50–80 Jewish detainees," it makes no sense to claim that "the crematorium had turned out to be too small and could not cope with the crema-

---

[178] German: *"der Krematorium,"* plural article, but singular noun.
[179] C. Mattogno, *Debunking the Bunkers of Auschwitz: Black Propaganda versus History*, 2nd ed., Castle Hill Publishers, Uckfield 2016.
[180] Otto Lenz, Ludwig Gaßner, *Schädlingsbekämpfung mit hochgiftigen Stoffen.* issue no. 1: "Blausäure," Verlagsbuchhandlung von Richard Schoetz, Berlin 1934, p. 15.

tions." This is a rather shaky argument for arranging that alleged gas chambers be built in the crematoria at Birkenau.

Finally, causing the victims to die within 30 seconds or one minute would have been an impossible task, even if using considerable quantities of Zyklon B. According to Haber's rule, a concentration of 1–2 g/m³ (hydrogen cyanide in air) is needed to kill a man in 30 to 60 seconds, the "immediately lethal" concentration being 0.3 g/m³.[181] However, according to a graph prepared by the Degesch Co. for the evaporation and diffusion of hydrogen cyanide, such concentrations are reached after 1.5 or 2.5 hours in the center of a room being gassed.[182] Thus, between a minimum of 1–2 minutes (close to the four points of introduction of Zyklon B) and a maximum of about one hour (in the farthest corner of the room) would have been needed for those concentrations of hydrogen cyanide to be attained.

In total, according to Aumeier, only four to five gassings were carried out in Crematorium I, and only from November or December 1942 on. Aumeier therefore squarely contradicts Filip Müller's account as to the period from May to November/December 1942.

3.5. Rudolf Höss

In his so-called Krakow notes, Rudolf Höss relates that in 1941 political commissars of the Red Army started to arrive who, on the basis of a secret order given by Himmler, were to be executed:[183]

"The first, smaller transports were executed by details taken from normal troops.

While [I was] away on a mission, my deputy, leader of the protective custody camp Fritzsch had used gas for killing. It was the hydrogen cyanide preparation Cyklon B, which was in constant use throughout the camp as a disinfestant and was readily available. After my return, he informed me about this, and the gas was used again for the next transport. The gassing was carried out in the prison cells of Block 11. I myself, protected by a gas-mask, have watched a gassing. In those cram-packed cells, death occurred immediately after [the

[181] Cf. C. Mattogno, *Olocausto: Dilettanti allo sbaraglio*. Edizioni di Ar, Padua 1996, pp. 185f. Editor's note: Executions in U.S. gas chambers using 3,200 ppm HCN (3.8 g/m³) last 10-15 minutes. To achieve death within a minute or faster, large quantities of soluble cyanide salts or liquid hydrogen cyanide have to be ingested. It is virtually impossible to kill within seconds by inhaling gaseous hydrogen cyanide. See Germar Rudolf, *The Rudolf Report*, 2nd ed., The Barnes Review, Washington, D.C., pp. 11f., 179-185, 193-201; cf. Fred A. Leuchter, Robert Faurisson, Germar Rudolf, *The Leuchter Reports. Critical Edition*, 4th ed., Castle Hill Publishers, Uckfield 2015, pp. 94-97.
[182] Deutsche Gesellschaft für Schädlingsbekämpfung m.b.H., *Fumigation Chambers for Pest Control*. Erasmus Druck Mainz, 1967, p. 9.
[183] Martin Broszat (ed.), *Kommandant in Auschwitz. Autobiographische Aufzeichnungen des Rudolf Höss*, Deutscher Taschenbuch Verlag, Munich 1981, p. 126.

gas] *was thrown in. Only a brief, almost suffocated screaming, and it was over. I did not become fully aware of this first gassing of people, I was perhaps too impressed by the whole process. I remember more vividly the gassing, a little later, of some 900 Russians in the old crematorium, since the use of Block 11 was too much of a hassle. While the unloading was going on, we simply broke a few holes through the earth and the concrete that constituted the roof of the morgue. The Russians had to undress in the vestibule and proceeded quietly into the morgue, as they had been told that they would all be deloused there. The whole transport would just fit into that morgue. The door was then locked and the gas dumped in through the openings. I don't know anymore how long this killing lasted. But for a while, one could hear this humming sound. Upon introduction, some of them yelled: 'Gas!,' then there was a lot of shouting, and they moved toward both doors, which, however, resisted the pressure. It was only several hours later that* [the room] *was opened and aired out."*

According to Danuta Czech, this gassing is supposed to have taken place on September 16, 1941,[184] but the only source the Polish historian offers is Höss, although he does not give any precise indication as to the date. It is certain from the documents,[185] though, that the first transports of Soviet POWs arrived at Auschwitz on October 6, 1941. This fact has been confirmed by Kazimierz Smoleń, ex-detainee of Auschwitz and later director of the Auschwitz Museum.[186] He was interned on July 6, 1940 (ID number 1327), and subsequently assigned to the Political Department, reporting to Maximilian Grabner. In his deposition of December 15, 1947, Smoleń declared:[187]

"In early October, the first transports of Russians came to Auschwitz."

Danuta Czech, on the other hand, basing herself on Höss's declarations, claims that 900 Soviet POWs were gassed on September 16, and another 600 on September 3 in the basement of Block 11.[188]

Höss affirms to have been present in person, wearing a gas mask, at a later gassing of Soviet prisoners in the basement of Block 11, but this gassing never took place according to the Auschwitz Museum. Commenting on Höss's assertion in this regard, an official text states:[189]

"It has not been possible to ascertain a second gassing of detainees in this block. Even though, here, Höss denies his presence at the first attempted killing by means of gas, he confirms it a few lines further on."

---

[184] D. Czech, *op. cit.* (note 82), p. 122.
[185] Cf. C. Mattogno, *op. cit.* (note 2), pp. 120-124.
[186] Cf. *ibid.*, pp. 117f.
[187] Sworn affidavit by K. Smoleń of December 15, 1947. NO-5849, p. 2.
[188] D. Czech, *op. cit.* (note 82), p. 117. This is said to be the famous "first gassing" at Auschwitz which, however, has no historical foundation.
[189] Jadwiga Bezwinska, Danuta Czech (eds.), *Auschwitz in den Augen der SS*, Staatliches Museum Auschwitz-Birkenau, 1997, note 107 on p. 64.

Thus Höss was either "present" at a gassing that took place in his absence, or else he was "present" at a gassing which never occurred!

Another surprising fact is that the agony of the victims of the first gassing, according to Polish sources, lasted an entire day – so long, in fact, that it was necessary for the SS to drop more Zyklon B into the cells the next day[190] – whereas in the gassing that Höss claims to have witnessed the deaths of the victims occurred "immediately upon introduction" of the gas. In another passage of his "notes," Höss writes that in the experiment conducted by Fritzsch – *i.e.* in the first gassing – the Zyklon B also provoked "the immediate death" of the victims.[191]

The description of the gassing in Crematorium I provided by Höss is, moreover, utterly grotesque. The morgue is said to have been chosen as a homicidal gas chamber at the very last minute in a decidedly improvised fashion. It was not equipped with gas-tight doors or with any ventilation,[192] or with openings for the introduction of Zyklon B, which were hastily made as the victims stepped down from the train!

The story of the gassing itself is even less believable. The Soviet prisoners allegedly undressed in the "vestibule" of the crematorium, which measured 4.14 by 7 = 28.9 m², and thus could accommodate 30 people at one time. Hence, the Soviet prisoners had to undress in 30 consecutive batches. They all "proceeded quietly into the morgue" because the SS had told them that they would be deloused there. In that morgue, however, there were no showers or other fake hygienic installations designed to fool the victims. Yet, nonetheless, the Soviet prisoners filed "quietly" into that room in groups of 30! In the end, there were 900 of them in a space of 78.2 square meters, *i.e.*, some 11 or 12 persons per square meter, but even then they did not suspect anything abnormal. It was only when the Zyklon B was introduced from the openings above that the obtuse victims realized they were going to be killed. Only then, Höss tries to tell us, did they try to break down the doors – but how could they have done so, wedged, as they were, 11 or 12 of them into the space of a telephone booth? They could hardly have moved an arm.

Finally, "only several hours later [the room...] was opened and aired out." This means, as we have already seen, that the crematorium, just like the basement room of Block 11, had to be ventilated for a couple of days, but then why was the gassing done in the crematorium?

It is important to note here that Höss never mentions a mechanical ventilation system for the morgue of Crematorium I. In the sentence just quot-

---

[190] Cf. C. Mattogno, *op. cit.* (note 2), pp. 92-94.

[191] Martin Broszat (ed.), *op. cit.* (note 183), p. 159.

[192] In September 1941, the morgue of the crematorium was still equipped with the makeshift ventilation system which the head of construction had installed at the end of February, but which was apparently unknown to Höss.

ed, he says "was opened and aired out," and not "was ventilated and opened" as would have been the case if a mechanical ventilation system had been available. In other words, according to Höss, the doors of the morgue were opened first and then, afterwards, a natural airing by draft took place.

At the March 12, 1947, session of his trial, when questioned about the first homicidal gassings at Auschwitz, Rudolf Höss declared:[193]

> *"After the first gassing in Block 11 – the building designated as a prison – transports were gassed in the old crematorium, in the so-called morgue. The gassing proceeded as follows: an opening was created in the ceiling, and through it the gas – a crystalline mass – was thrown into the room. I remember only one transport. It comprised 900 POWs who were gassed in this way. From then on, gassing was done outside the camp, in 'Bunker 1.'"*

Hence, according to the commandant of Auschwitz, the alleged gas chamber of Crematorium I, which according to him had only one opening for the introduction of Zyklon B, was used only until the so-called Bunker 1 was said to have been ready, *i.e.* until January 1942.[194]

3.6. Pery Broad

Former SS-*Rottenführer* Pery Broad was transferred to Auschwitz on April 8, 1942. He was assigned to the Political Department on June 18, reporting to SS-*Untersturmführer* Maximilian Grabner. Broad was arrested by the British on May 6, 1945, and released in 1947. On July 13, 1945, he drew up a report which was never registered by any "commission for the investigation of the German war crimes," and therefore never received any registration number. It thus disappeared completely for around 20 years and then suddenly resurfaced at the Auschwitz trial in Frankfurt.

On April 20, 1964, during the 39th session, a certain Hermann Rothmann was questioned and made the following statement: At the end of the war he worked at the Intelligence Section of the British government. Broad, who was working in the same office as an interpreter, handed him his now famous report on Auschwitz in six copies. Rothmann kept one for himself and later handed it over to the Frankfurt tribunal.[195]

Another witness, Cornelis van het Kaar, likewise employed by the British secret service at the time, declared that in June 1945 Broad had volunteered the story of the Auschwitz camp to him. Van het Kaar asked Broad

---

[193] AGK, NTN, 105, pp. 110f.
[194] D. Czech, "Kalendarium der Ereignisse im Konzentrationslager Auschwitz-Birkenau," in: *Hefte von Auschwitz,* Wydawnictwo Państwowego Muzeum w Oświęcimiu, issue 3, 1960, p. 49.
[195] H. Langbein, *op. cit.* (note 91), *op. cit.*, p. 537.

to write down his experience at Auschwitz, and Broad then handed to the British a written report around June 15.[196] When questioned about the report during the Frankfurt trial, Broad declared:[195]

> *"In 1945 I wrote a report on Auschwitz, which I handed to the English in the British camp of Munsterlager. A copy of my report was prepared there. I have leafed through the photocopy presented to me here. Some parts are my text, some parts seem to have been added by others, some parts, too, are wrong. I am surprised that such things are attributed to me."*

After having read the report, Broad said:[197]

> *"Certain sections I recognize to be my own notes, but not the document in its entirety."*

It is certainly true that Broad accepted those parts of the report which speak of the gassings as authentic,[197] but it is also true that his situation in the trial increasingly worsened, to the point that during the hearing of November 6, 1964 – having hitherto been present in freedom – he was arrested immediately after the deposition of a certain Ota Fabian, who accused him of having murdered various detainees.[198] Broad then lodged a motion with the court in which he claimed to have done nothing of the kind.[199]

Obviously, Broad was trying to mollify the court and had no wish to alienate it by contesting the parts of his report which were essential for the trial. It is certain, however, that the report presented to the Frankfurt tribunal, which was later published in its entirety by the Auschwitz Museum,[200] had been manipulated. The strangest aspect is that neither Broad nor the two British agents mentioned above gave a precise date for the report: the date is, in fact, known only because Broad mentioned it in a sworn statement to the British at Minden on December 14, 1945.[201] In that statement he also quotes two passages of his report (concerning the alleged homicidal gassing in Crematorium I at which he claimed to have been present), which on the whole correspond to the text published by the Auschwitz Museum.

In a later sworn statement, dated October 20, 1947, Broad describes the alleged gassing. He asserts that in May 1942 SS-*Hauptscharführer* Hössler formed a special SS unit that was ordered to close off all roads leading to the crematorium. Broad continues:[202]

---

[196] *Ibid.*, p. 538.
[197] *Ibid.*, p. 539.
[198] *Ibid.*, p. 528.
[199] *Ibid.*, p. 541.
[200] Pery Broad, "KZ-Auschwitz. Erinnerungen eines SS-Mannes der Politischen Abteilung in dem Konzentrationslager Auschwitz," in: *Hefte von Auschwitz*. Wydawnictwo Państwowego Muzeum w Oświęcimiu, 9, 1966, pp. 7-48.
[201] NI-11937.
[202] NI-11984.

"A few weeks later, the offices of the Political Department, which at the time were located on the lower floor of the infirmary, were cleared in the early morning hours and the personnel sent to their lodgings. I did not follow this order, but hid in the upper part of the stairwell. From there, I could observe the crematorium, which was some 100 m away.[203] *After some time, the high entrance gate that led to the vestibule was opened, and a group of some 200 persons was led through by some SS men whose names I do not know. Then the gate was closed again. I could not observe what went on in the yard, because the gate and the enclosure were too high.*

Then Untersturmführer Grabner and another SS man whom I do not remember appeared on the roof of the crematorium and gave instructions to the people assembled in the yard, which, however, I could not understand. A few minutes later, two more SS men, wearing gas masks, stepped onto the roof of the crematorium. They opened the six aeration traps that were located in the flat roof, opened several tin cans by hitting them with a hammer, poured the contents through the openings, and closed them again. While they did all this, the engine of a truck standing in front of the crematorium was running, probably in order to drown out the screams of the people dying. About 5 minutes later the action was finished, the truck moved away, and the access roads were again opened to traffic. These measures were repeated several times in the Auschwitz crematorium during 1942, but I was no longer able to observe them."

The description of the alleged homicidal gassing is much more detailed in the "Broad Report," but also very contradictory. There one can read that the unit set up by Hössler did not wait "several weeks" before blocking the roads leading to the crematorium, but did so immediately after it had been formed.[204] The victims were not "a group of some 200 people," but "300 to 400 people."

Broad never explains from where he observed this, how far he was away from the events, and the scenes segue like in a movie. For example, he describes, with a wealth of details, the unloading of this transport at the old ramp, which was located between Auschwitz and Birkenau, and which was certainly not visible from the stairwell of the hospital! Then the scene changes to the victims – Jews – whose appearance Broad describes with much attention; from what they say, he finally learns that they had been operating machines in a factory.[204] Then the victims step into the yard of the crematorium, and the gate closes on them. At this point, Grabner, with Hössler, climbs up on the roof of the crematorium and gives a speech – the one which Broad, from his post, had not been able to hear, but which he reports faithfully nonetheless:[205]

---

[203] The actual distance is 20 meters.
[204] Pery Broad, *op. cit.* (note 200), p. 30.
[205] *Ibid.*, p. 31.

"You will now be bathed and disinfected so we will not have any epidemics in the camp. Then you will go to your lodgings, where hot soup is waiting for you, and you will be put to work according to your professions. Take your clothes off here in the yard and put them on the ground in front of you."

In his previous statement, Broad asserted that he "could not observe what went on in the yard, because the gate and the enclosure were too high," but in the "Report" he diligently records the reactions of the victims in the yard: for example "some of them were looking forward to the hot soup" promised by Grabner.[205] After mentioning a conversation between Grabner and the victims on the subject of the alleged showers in the crematorium, Broad describes the way they entered the morgue of the crematorium, giving the impression that he was among them:[205]

"The first ones moved through the vestibule into the morgue. Everything is spotless. Only the strange odor is intimidating to a few of them. In vain they look at the ceiling in their search for showerheads or water pipes."

The doors are closed, and the victims become aware of the deception. From his position Broad clearly sees what is happening in the "gas chamber":[205]

"They pound on the door, hammer it with their fists in their desperate fury. Cynical laughs are the answer they receive."

With a final effort, Broad manages to hear the reply of the SS:[205]

"'Don't scald yourselves when you take your bath,' someone yells through the door."

Broad then goes on – as if he were in the "gas chamber" himself:[205]

"Some of them notice that the covers of the six holes in the ceiling are being taken off."

Then the scene changes to the outside of the crematorium, and Broad describes how the disinfestors pour Zyklon B through the holes in the roof of the crematorium. At that moment, the engine of the truck is started up, but in spite of its roar, Broad again manages to hear the screams of the victims, which after two minutes turn into a subdued moan.[206] Then, still looking through the walls, he sees the unit of detainees at work in the crematorium and observes the corpses as they stand, one leaning against the next, "with their mouths wide open."[207]

Broad concludes his narrative with the following assertion:[206]

"One transport after another vanished into the Auschwitz crematorium. Every day! There were more and more victims, and the murder had to be organized

---

[206] *Ibid.*, pp. 32f.
[207] *Ibid.*, p. 32.

on a larger scale. The morgue could not take in enough. Cremation of the corpses took too long."

Therefore, the alleged mass extermination is said to have been moved to the so-called "Bunkers" of Birkenau.

On March 2, 1946, Pery Broad testified in the Tesch trial and again spoke about the alleged gassing in Crematorium I of Auschwitz:[208]

"In July 1942 I was in the neighbourhood of the SS infirmary about 40 to 45 metres[209] from the Auschwitz crematorium, and there I saw, for the first time, a gassing."

Thus, he was not inside the building but in its vicinity!

Broad went on to say that in the flat roof of the crematorium there were "six holes of the diameter of ten centimeters."[208] Hence, the openings for the introduction of Zyklon B had a diameter smaller than the standard size of the Zyklon B cans, which was 15.4 centimeters![210]

When asked about the frequency of gassings in the crematorium, Broad replied:[208]

"I cannot say for certain, because I have seen only that one, but I could draw my conclusions about different gassing actions, because a concentration [sic] of several guards would be concentrated by Untersturmführer Hurstler [Hössler] once or twice per month."

The gassings in the old crematorium thus occurred once or twice per month, but in the "Broad Report" it is said that they took place "every day"! But this is not the end of the ludicrous stories from this self-styled eyewitness. When questioned about the capacity of the Birkenau crematoria, Broad answered:[208]

"In Crematoriums 1 and 2, 3,000 to 4,000. In crematoriums 3 and 4, 2,000. In No. 5 there was only a gas stove there – 800 to 1200."

Actually, besides the four crematoria (designated II–V), a fifth crematorium never existed at Birkenau, and there was never "a gas stove"!

The cremation capacity indicated by the witness is sheer nonsense: for a period of 24 hours, the theoretical maximum cremation capacity was 300 bodies each for Crematoria II and III, and 180 each for Crematoria IV and V.[211] With respect to the 3 double-muffle furnaces of Crematorium I, Broad says only that "4 to 6 corpses at one time"[212] were cremated there, which is a similar aberration, to say nothing of the "fiery flame several me-

---

[208] NI-11954.
[209] The text erroneously has "kilometers"!
[210] The 500-gram can was 12.5 cm high, the 1,500-gram can 31.5 centimeters.
[211] C. Mattogno, *The Cremation Furnaces of Auschwitz, op. cit.* (note 38), p. 337.
[212] Pery Broad, *op. cit.* (note 200), p 19.

ters high," which he claimed to have seen coming out regularly from the chimney of the crematorium![213]

When he was asked to make an estimate of the number of those gassed during his tour of duty at Auschwitz, he stated:[208]

"I would think 2½ million to 3 million."

Pery Broad thus stuck without hesitation to the prosecution's absurd theses, and it is clear that such a person would have "confessed" to anything in order to please his captors.

Actually, the story of the alleged gassing in Crematorium I in July 1942 does not jibe well with the known history of the crematorium, since outside work was carried out at the crematorium during the second half of May: The front yard was fenced in and given two wooden access gates, 4 m wide and 3.20 m high, and the old pavement was replaced.[214]

Between June 12 and August 8, 1942, the crematorium was one vast worksite engaging hundreds of people – 688 detainees and 123 civilian workers – who demolished the old chimney and built a new one with new flues. There was a constant coming and going of trucks bringing in tons and tons of material – 31 tons of refractory brick alone![215] – and carting off tons and tons of rubble from the old chimney.

There is not the least reference in Pery Broad's account to this feverish activity, which is very telling. No one can seriously believe that under these circumstances, with civilian workers all over the place, even in the furnace hall, the camp SS would have organized one or more homicidal gassings in the crematorium. And that, when at the same time they allegedly had the two gassing "Bunkers" at their disposal, much more spacious and much better shielded from indiscreet observers.

Besides, if we follow Danuta Czech's *Kalendarium*, there was no homicidal gassing during the second half of May of 1942,[216] and only a single one between June 1 and 12 (beginning of the work on the chimney), which, however, is said to have taken place on June 2 in the alleged "Bunker"1.[217]

---

[213] *Ibid.*, p. 20. Cf. in this respect my article "Flames and Smoke from the Chimneys of Crematoria," *The Revisionist*, 2(1) (2004), pp. 73-78.

[214] *"Zentralbauleitung, Auftrag Nr. 436, Arbeitskarte Nr. 20 for Tischlerei"* of May 13, 1942: fabrication of two entrance gates (*Einfahrttore*) 4×3,20 m, work done between May 21 and 25. RGVA, 502-2-1, p. 24. Description of work done: *"Tätigkeitsbericht für den Monat Mai 1942,"* RGVA, 502-1-24, p. 299, and *"Baubericht für Monat Mai 1942,"* RGVA, 502-1-24, p. 261.

[215] Handwritten note *"Schornstein-Krematorium. BW 11"* of December 7, 1942. RGVA, 502-1-318, pp. 4f.

[216] The alleged gassing cannot have taken place before May 25, 1942, because that was the completion date of the two entrance gates (*Einfahrttore*) to the crematorium yard, one of which is mentioned by Pery Broad in his account.

[217] D. Czech, *op. cit.* (note 82), pp. 213-226.

In conclusion, the "gassing" described by Pery Broad cannot have taken place while the work on the chimneys was going on, or during the two weeks previous, and therefore it never took place.

3.7. Maximilian Grabner

Maximilian Grabner, initially a detective with the criminal investigation department of the Vienna police, later with the State Police at Kattowitz, was transferred to Auschwitz in June 1940 and became head of the Political Department of the camp, with the rank of SS-*Unterscharführer*. In December 1943, he was arrested for unlawful appropriation of inmate property (embezzlement) and sentenced to 12 years' imprisonment by an SS tribunal.

According to Pery Broad, who was one of his subordinates, Grabner was the organizer and supervisor of the alleged homicidal gassings in the morgue of Crematorium I and should, therefore, have been excellently informed about them.

He was arrested by the Vienna Gestapo on August 3, 1945.[218] After several days, the police started to question the witnesses against him. One of the first was Hermann Langbein, an ex-detainee of Auschwitz and future historian of the camp, who declared:[219]

"Of course Grabner was present at the mass gassings of transports that came to Auschwitz. In the course of these transports, some 5,000,000 [sic!] people were gassed."

On September 1, 1945, Grabner was interrogated. Regarding the beginning of the alleged gassings at Auschwitz, he declared:[220]

"Starting in early 1942, detainees at Auschwitz were murdered by means of gas; to be precise, it started in Block 11. I have myself seen these gassings; the SS was walking around with gas masks; the detainees, 20–40 men [at a time], were herded into the cells. Then the cells were sealed and filled with gas."

In a declaration dated September 26, 1945, Grabner furnished more details:[221]

---

[218] *"Staatspolizei Wien, Haftbefehl Nr. 1619. Wien, am 3. August 1945."* GARF, 7021-108-34, p. 12.
[219] Interrogation of Hermann Langbein, Vienna, August 8, 1945. GARF, 7021-108-34, p. 22.
[220] Minutes of the declarations of Maximilian Grabner, Vienna, September 1, 1945. GARF, 7021-108-34, p. 26.
[221] Minutes of the declarations of Maximilian Grabner, Vienna, September 26, 1945. APMO, Proces załogi, vol. 53, p. 65.

"Furthermore, 2,000 Russians – probably partisans – who had been held in the bunker [basement prison] of Block 11 completely isolated from the rest of the camp, were gassed in two groups of 1,000 each."

In his declaration of September 17, 1947, he asserted that this had been the first experimental gassing.[222] As we have seen, though, the "first gassing" in the basement of Block 11 has no historical foundation. Moreover, if we follow the orthodox historians, only one gassing, not two, was carried out in Block 11.

Grabner's account is fairly unbelievable: he claims that 2,000 Russians were held in the prison cells of the Bunker in Block 11. However, the total surface area of the 28 cells in that basement is roughly 238 square meters,[223] which means that the Russians would have been kept in cells holding $(2,000 \div 238=)$ 8 persons per square meter! Then 1,000 Russians would have been moved out (where?), and the 1,000 remaining would have been gassed in their cells, after making them gas-tight – but then how could the gas have been introduced into the cells?

Grabner went on to talk about the crematorium of Auschwitz:[224]

"Later the gassings were carried out in the old crematorium, across from the SS infirmary. Aside from detainees selected for this purpose, people were brought in by the police, the Gestapo, or the Wehrmacht. Holes were drilled into the concrete ceiling of the bunker,[225] *through which the gas (Ziklon) [sic] was fed in. The bunker had a capacity of 700–800 people. Next to the bunker was the crematorium, in which the dead were burned immediately. Several times a week there were such gassings. There were detainees working in the old crematorium who had been selected for this detail and who had to help with the gassing. After a while, this detail was itself gassed and replaced by new detainees."*

In the declaration of September 12, 1945, Grabner added:[226]

"I declare that in the period of 1941/1942 alone, 300,000 dead were buried at the same time (within a short period of time), because the capacity of the small crematorium was not adequate for the numbers of dead. Long trenches were dug, and those [trenches] filled up with corpses. In connection with the propaganda about Katyn, an order came from Berlin in 1942 to unearth the corpses and to burn them, so as to leave no traces. A unit of several hundred detainees was assigned to this task; the unearthed corpses had started to rot and were partly decomposed. At the site and all around there was such filthy odor that I did not like being at that location. After this was done, the detainees were gassed."

---

[222] APMO, Proces załogi, vol. 53b, p. 358.
[223] C. Mattogno, *op. cit.* (note 2), p. 29.
[224] Minutes…, *op. cit.* (note 220), p. 26.
[225] This refers to the morgue of the crematorium.
[226] Minutes of the declarations of Maximilian Grabner, Vienna, September 12, 1945, p. 25.

We would thus be dealing here with the alleged gassing of the *"Sonder-kommando"* in Crematorium I in December 1942, about which the alleged perpetrator, Maximilian Grabner, knew practically nothing!

The story of the 300,000 buried corpses has no foundation in fact: not even Rudolf Höss went that far. He was satisfied with a more modest figure of 107,000 corpses,[227] but this figure, too, is pure fantasy.

The reference to Katyn is completely out of place, because the graves with the remains of the Polish soldiers murdered by the Soviets were discovered by the Germans on April 13, 1943, whereas at Auschwitz the unearthing and burning of the corpses is said to have started on September 21, 1942.[228] It is curious – but only at first glance – that Pery Broad, too, should have adopted the same motive for the exhumation of the corpses in the mass graves:[229]

> *"In view of Katyn, one could not take the liberty of having such mass graves, in which the corpses apparently would not decompose and which would, moreover, reappear eventually."*

This agreement on an impossible point in two independent testimonies, since it could not stem from the witnesses, demonstrates that it must have come from the interrogators who were questioning them. In other words, here, as in all the concordances and convergences that Robert Jan van Pelt has found in independent testimonies, the information simply reflects all the commonplace facets of the propaganda "truth" about Auschwitz that were in circulation at the time.

But back to Grabner. His description of the first homicidal gassings is generic and superficial, and cannot be the fruit of any real and direct experience. One cannot even say that he was reluctant to "confess" – quite the opposite. Even more so than Pery Broad, he prostituted himself in the cause of his accusers, "confessing" the most absurd charges.

In the declaration of September 12, 1945, mentioned above, he affirms that the victims at Auschwitz amounted to "at least three million," for the period during which he was the head of the Political Department, *i.e.*, up to the end of 1943 alone![226] (In this declaration the figure of three million victims appears no less than three times!) But earlier, in the statement of September 1, 1945, he even had gone so far as to say:[230]

> *"While I was in charge of the political department at Auschwitz, some 3 to 6,000,000 people were murdered in this or a similar fashion."*

Grabner's line of defense was decidedly childish: the whole responsibility for the alleged mass extermination was that of the camp commandant, Ru-

---

[227] Martin Broszat (ed.), *op. cit.* (note 183), p. 161.
[228] D. Czech, *op. cit.* (note 82), p. 305.
[229] Pery Broad, *op. cit.* (note 200), p. 27.
[230] Minutes..., *op. cit.* (note 220), p. 26a.

dolf Höss, whom Grabner described as a merciless and blood-thirsty man. He – Grabner – had not only committed no crime, but he had tried in every way possible to help the detainees and to sabotage the activity of those "bandits" of Auschwitz. His verbose declaration of September 17, 1947, at which point in time he was in the hands of the Poles, is a tedious account of his alleged good deeds at Auschwitz.[231] Among these there are some that are so fatuous that is worthwhile mentioning them here:[232]

> *"Of the four crematoria of Birkenau, I have intentionally damaged the two large ones that stood in the forest,[233] causing them to be shut down for a while. Secretly, I had poured used engine oil into the chimney."*

The Crematoria IV and V each had two chimneys 16.87 m high. Each chimney was connected to half the furnace, *i.e.*, to four muffles. The chimneys had no man-holes. They rose above the roof of the crematoria, and their mouths could be reached by means of a ladder consisting of 25 iron steps anchored in the masonry.[234] We can see Grabner secretly climbing upon the roof of Crematorium IV by means of a ladder, with two buckets full of engine oil under his arm, then crawling and coughing his way up the iron steps to the top of the chimney with one of the buckets in one of his hands, pouring the oil into the chimney, climbing down again to repeat the feat on the other chimney and then doing a repeat performance at Crematorium V! And all this to achieve nothing at all, since oil poured into a chimney simply doesn't do anything to it.

But those were not the only (alleged) deeds of sabotage which Grabner undertook. He goes on to say:[232]

> *"Earlier, I had brought the small crematorium[235] to a standstill. At the point where it meets the stack, I likewise poured a bucket of oil into the air shaft, with the result that the first time it cracked and the second time it blew up altogether, including the furnaces."*

In reality, there was no air shaft in the crematorium. Until the end of 1943, the chimneys and flues of Crematorium II, the chimney and the 8-muffle furnace of Crematorium IV, and, as we have already seen, the chimney of Crematorium I did suffer damage – well documented, by the way – but not because of any acts of sabotage, whether by Grabner or anyone else.

No less ridiculous is Grabner's assertion that, had he collaborated in the alleged mass gassings, he would have been granted a special leave of 3 to 6

---

[231] Minutes of the declarations of Maximilian Grabner, Krakow, September 17, 1947. APMO, Proces załogi, vol. 53, pp. 293-332.
[232] *Ibid.*, p. 300.
[233] Crematoria IV and V, which were the small ones, however.
[234] The steps are clearly visible on the photograph of Crematorium V published by J.-C. Pressac, *op. cit.* (note 33), p. 419.
[235] Crematorium I of Auschwitz.

weeks in Italy at the expense of the Reich, plus an allowance of 300 to 600 Reichsmark.[236]

When it comes to the history of the Auschwitz Camp, Grabner's credibility is characterized by the following sentence:[237]

> *"1940. At the end of April, the Auschwitz camp is set up as an extermination camp by an order from Berlin."*

We have here another example of the propaganda of the period, disguised as truth, together with the figure of 3, 5 or 6 million victims.

Maximilian Grabner thus not only accepted whole-heartedly the lies of his accusers on the subject of what had happened at Auschwitz, but in a sort of masochistic frenzy added some of his own that were even more blatant. In doing so, he perhaps hoped to avoid being extradited to Poland. He had, after all, a wife, three small children, and an aging mother. Instead, he became one of the most prominent among the defendants during the trial of the camp garrison and was sentenced to death on December 22, 1947, and subsequently executed.

3.8. Hans Stark

SS-*Unterscharführer* Hans Stark served at Auschwitz from Christmas 1940 to November 1942, with an extended furlough from Christmas 1941 until the end of March 1942. In June 1941 he joined the Political Department.[238] In the summer of 1942 he was made *Oberscharführer*. On April 23, 1959, he was interrogated by the *Landeskriminalamt* Baden-Württemberg during the preparation of the Frankfurt trial. On that occasion, he declared:[239]

> *"As early as the autumn of 1941 gassings were carried out in a room of the small crematorium, the room having been fitted for that purpose. It could take in some 200–250 people, was higher than a normal living room, had no windows, and only one door that had been made [gas] tight and had a lock like the door of an air-raid shelter. There were no pipes or anything which could have led the detainees to believe they were in a shower room. In the ceiling, a certain distance apart, there were two openings with a diameter of about 35 centimeters. This room had a flat roof, which caused daylight to enter through these openings. The granular Zyklon B was poured in through the openings. The Zyklon B was stored in the SS infirmary and was used for disinfection purposes. Who it was that had hit on the idea of using this product for the gassing*

---

[236] Minutes…, *op. cit.* (note 231), p. 321.
[237] Minutes…, *op. cit.* (note 221), p. 63.
[238] Staatsanwaltschaft…, *op. cit.* (note 132), vol. VI, pp. 939, 942.
[239] Minutes of interrogation of Hans Stark, Cologne, April 23, 1959. ZStL, ref. AR-Z 37/58 SB6, pp. 947-949.

of people I do not know, but it was rumored among the camp SS personnel that in the fall of 1941 the product had been tried out for the first time for the gassing of detainees in a cell of Block 11. I do not know who had ordered and carried out this test, but it was said the that leader of the protective custody camp Fritzsch had been present. I do not know any details.

As I have already said, the first gassing in the small crematorium was carried out in the fall of 1941. As with the shootings, I was requested by Grabner to come to the crema in order to check the number. Initially, I did not know that there was to be a gassing. Near the crema there were some 200–250 Jewish men, women, and children; babies may have been among them, all ages. Without being able to give any names, I can say that quite a number of SS personnel were present – the camp commandant, the leader of the protective custody camp, several block leaders, Grabner, and other members of the Political Department. The Jews were not told anything; they were simply requested to enter the gassing room, the door of which stood open. While the Jews were entering the room, medics prepared the gassing. Earth had been banked up to ceiling level against one of the outside walls of the gassing room so that they could get on top of the room. Once all the Jews were in the room, it was bolted, and the medics poured the Zyklon B into the openings. I do not remember how many cans of Zyklon B were used, but it was more than one. I cannot give the names of the medics. […]

At a later gassing – still in the autumn of 1941 – I received an order from Grabner to pour Zyclon B into the opening, because only one medic had come, and it was necessary for a gassing to pour Zyclon B into both openings at the same time. This gassing, again, concerned a transport of 200–250 Jews, and again there were men, women, and children. As I have already stated, this Zyclon B was granular, and thus it would run down over the people when it was being poured in. They then started to scream terribly, for they now knew what was happening to them. I did not look down through the opening because the openings had to be closed immediately once the Zyclon B had been introduced. A few minutes later, it was quiet. After some time, perhaps 10–15 minutes, the gassing room was opened. The dead people lay every which way, it was a dreadful sight. The detainee unit of the crema then took the gassed into the crema.

On account of my job as head of the registration department, I was thus present at each gassing or shooting. How many people were killed in my presence during that period, I cannot say. I cannot say either, how many gassings were carried out in my presence. It was roughly the same number of persons each time."

Hans Stark indicated that in the alleged gas chamber of Crematorium I only Jews were gassed:[240]

---

[240] *Ibid.*, p. 955.

> *"During the gassings, which, as already indicated, had started as early as the autumn of 1941 and at which I was present, only Jews were gassed; to be precise, they were always new arrivals."*

At the Auschwitz trial, Stark comes back to the alleged homicidal gassings:[241]

> *"Stark: Grabner told me there would be a transport and I should be ready. The transport had been announced for the evening, sometime between 20 and 21 hours, but it arrived only around 22 hours. Then it turned out that those were not people to be registered but people that had been sentenced to death by a court-martial. The commandant ordered them to be taken to the small crematorium to be gassed there.*
> *Presiding judge: How many were there?*
> *S: I do not know. There may have been 150 or 200 of them. After all, it was 4 truckloads. It was Jews and Poles.*
> *PJ: Women too?*
> *S: Yes sir, also.*
> *PJ: Children too?*
> *S: No children were coming to Auschwitz in 1941. The lists were compared and once they had been read out, we moved on to the small crematorium.*
> *PJ: What were the detainees told?*
> *S: Nothing, they were already informed.*
> *PJ: Informed about what?*
> *S: That they would be shot. Once all were inside, the man on top who was responsible for the gassing got ready. Usually, two people were needed. But he was alone. He called down that he needed another one. I was the only one who was still standing around in the group of leaders present; the others were busy in the gassing room. So Grabner said: 'Go and help!' I did not move right away. Then the leader of the protective custody camp came up and said: 'Get moving!' and the commandant said: 'If you do not climb up there, you will be put in with the others.' So I had to go up and help the man above pour."*

The alleged first homicidal gassing in Crematorium I took place, according to Stark, in October 1941,[242] but that date is at variance with the one given by Czech (September 16, 1941). As far as the alleged gas chamber is concerned, Stark says only that it had "one door that had been made especially tight", but the morgue had two doors (see Chapter 6.1.). He speaks of "two openings with a diameter of about 35 centimeters"– hence they were round – which squarely contradicts Broad's data: six square openings 10 by 10 centimeters. The victims were "only Jews," whereas according to Rudolf Höss they were only Soviet prisoners of war.

The gassing, in which Stark claimed to have directly participated, concerned "200–250 Jews" or, likewise, "150 or 200 [...] Jews and Poles"; the

---

[241] H. Langbein, *op. cit.* (note 91), pp. 438f.
[242] *Ibid.*, p. 438.

victims were gassed for being Jews and, at the same time, because they were "people that had been sentenced to death by a court-martial." In this connection, there obviously were no "children," but then, on the other hand, the victims were "men, women, and children."

The witness claims to have been present at each gassing in his capacity of "head of the registration department," his specific task being to check the number of victims, yet he was unable to say anything about the total number of victims of the alleged gassings, or about the number of gassings carried out in his presence!

Stark claims that the gassings had to be carried out by pouring Zyklon B through the two openings at the same time. Why at the same time? Was there any need for this? None at all. We have here, in fact, a simple literary maneuver resorted to by Stark in order to introduce the story of his participation in a homicidal gassing against his will, under threat of death from the commandant himself. Such cheap shenanigans on the part of the accused, which did not do him any harm, enabled him to show a "cooperative" attitude, and were aimed at mollifying the judges.

Another detail of his pre-trial deposition which has nothing to do with Crematorium I also points to the fact that Stark was indeed lying:[243] He reported about homicidal gassings in two wooden houses erected in early 1942 close to the railway ramp at Birkenau.[244] Yet Stark was not even present in that camp in early 1942, the railway ramp at Birkenau was built only in 1944, and such wooden gassing houses are otherwise completely unheard of.

That Stark's memory was highly unreliable also results from the fact that he identified scenes in "photos shown to me about the selections at the arrival of transports [of Jews at the railway ramp in Birkenau in 1944]" as "the situation as it really occurred […]." [245] Yet the photos shown to him depicted the situation of the camp in May 1944, that is to say, one and a half years after his departure from Auschwitz in November 1942. The ramp shown on those photos didn't exist back then. Hence Stark related in his depositions at least to some degree not what he had personally experience at Auschwitz, but what he had learned about it after the war. This is confirmed by a remark of his pre-trial interrogator in the investigation files, according to which Stark admitted to always having eagerly consumed media items about Auschwitz.[246]

Since Stark wasn't even 21 years of age at the time of the alleged crime, he was indicted and sentenced under juvenile law. Of course he knew this,

---

[243] Cf. G. Rudolf, "From the Records of the Frankfurt Auschwitz Trial, Part 7," *The Revisionist* 3(1) (2005), pp. 92-97, here pp. 94-97.
[244] Staatsanwaltschaft…, *op. cit.* (note 132), pp. 949-951.
[245] *Ibid.*, p. 951.
[246] *Ibid.*, p. 962.

and he knew also that his "confessions," no matter how terrible and fantastic they might be, could lead to no more than 10 years of imprisonment. And indeed, he was eventually sentenced to no more than ten years in prison for at least 44 instances of murder, committed together with others. Some three years after the pronouncement of the verdict, Stark's prison term was already over.[247]

---

[247] H. Langbein, *op. cit.* (note 91), p. 885; cf. http://en.wikipedia.org/wiki/Hans_Stark

Chapter 4:
The Historians

4.1. Danuta Czech

The second German edition of the Auschwitz *Kalendarium* has only two entries relating to alleged homicidal gassings in Crematorium I. They are considered highly significant because they pinpoint the first gassing (of Soviet POWs) and the beginning of the gassings of Jews.

The first entry is for September 16, 1941. Danuta Czech writes:[248]

> *"900 Russian prisoners of war are killed with gas. The killing by gas takes place in the morgue of the crematorium, because the use of the cellars in Block 11 would have been too cumbersome."*

In a note, the Polish writer explains:[248]

> *"This probably occurred in September, for Höss writes, in his notes [...]"*

Czech then quotes the passage concerning the alleged gassing of 900 Soviet POWs, said to have followed the gassing conducted in the basement of Block 11, about which Höss declares that he observed it as an "eyewitness," but which, in the end, the Auschwitz Museum considers never to have taken place. Höss gives no dates for those events, merely placing them in the autumn of 1941. From this vague indication, Danuta Czech – one does not quite know by which hermeneutical stroke of genius – comes up with the precise date of September 16, 1941, even though, as I have explained above, the first Soviet POWs arrived at Auschwitz only in early October.

The second entry concerns the date of February 15, 1942:[249]

> *"The first transport of Jews arrives from Beuthen. They have been arrested by the Stapoleitstelle [Gestapo marshalling center] and are destined to be killed at Auschwitz concentration camp. They are unloaded at the platform of the camp railway spur. They have to leave their luggage on the platform. The camp's on duty takes over the deportees from the Stapo and leads them to the gas chamber located in the camp crematorium. There they are killed with Zyklon B."*

The sources given by Czech are Höss and Broad. However, the first gassing of Jews mentioned by the ex-commandant of Auschwitz took place, as

---

[248] D. Czech, *op. cit.* (note 82), p. 122.
[249] *Ibid.*, pp. 174f.

he puts it, "probably still in September 1941, but possibly only in January 1942";[250] what's more, that gassing was not carried out in Crematorium I, but in "Bunker" I:[251]

> *"At the platform, the Jews were taken over by the camp's staff on duty from the Stapo and then taken, in two sections, by the leader of the protective custody camp to the Bunker, as the extermination facility was called. [...] Near the Bunker, the Jews had to undress. They were told that for delousing they had to enter the rooms so labelled. All rooms, five altogether,[252] were filled at the same time, the gas-tight doors were screwed shut and the contents of the gas cans dumped into the rooms through special hatches."*

As we have already seen, Broad claims to have been present at a single gassing in Crematorium I, but according to him this was in July 1942.

Thus, from a gassing allegedly carried out in "Bunker 1" at some time between September 1941 and January 1942, and from another gassing claimed to have taken place in Crematorium I, but in July of 1942, Czech deduces that this gassing occurred on February 15, 1942, in Crematorium I!

This is not really surprising, as such sloppy methods are typical of Czech. I have demonstrated elsewhere, by what deceptive practices she came up with a fantastic account of the "first gassing" in the basement of Block 11 at Auschwitz, when she pieced together fragments of testimonies which are contradictory in all respects.[253]

4.2. J.-C. Pressac (1989)

As I have already noted, Jean-Claude Pressac is the first scholar to have tried to bring the story of the gassings in the morgue of Crematorium I back into the realm of historiography. In his first work on Auschwitz, he calls this crematorium "a powerful symbol," because it served two functions:

> *"First, its present role of being the only Auschwitz Krematorium where a gas chamber can be visited,"*

and, second, its historical role as a "test bed" for the gassings and cremations in Crematoria II and III. He admits that the documents (known to him at the time) "do not make it possible to formally establish proof of homicidal gassing in its morgue," and that one therefore has to resort to testimo-

---

[250] Martin Broszat (ed.), *op. cit.* (note 183), pp. 159f.
[251] *Ibid.*, p. 160.
[252] According to orthodox historiography, "Bunker 1" had only two rooms.
[253] Cf. the section "Danuta Czech's Historiographic Method," in: C. Mattogno, *op. cit.* (note 2), pp. 86-88.

nies of eyewitnesses.[254] He examines four witnesses: Alter Fajnzylberg, Filip Müller, Rudolf Höss, and Pery Broad.

As for the first witness, he analyzes the sworn declaration of September 29, 1980, and an excerpt of the deposition of April 16, 1945. The other three witnesses are given only very little space by Pressac.

From Filip Müller's statements he discusses only the detail of the crematorium chimney – round according to the witness, square according to the German documents available then.[255] And that is all.

Pressac devotes eight lines to Rudolf Höss. He finds that "two details are unlikely" in his account:[256]

"The squeezing of 900 persons in 78,2 m² and the 'rapid' drilling of several holes in the ceiling to pour the Zyclon-B. Drilling through 10 to 15 cm of concrete was not a job that could be done on the spur of the moment."

The French historian explains these improbabilities by saying that "he [Höss] was present without seeing."[256]

In the eleven lines that he dedicates to Pery Broad, Pressac states that "the form and tone of his declaration sound false" and that "its present literary form is visibly coloured by a rather too flagrant Polish patriotism" and finally that "the original manuscript of his declaration is not known," but this declaration still has to be accepted, because either Broad has adopted "the language of the victor," as Pierre Vidal-Naquet put it, or his declaration has been "slightly" retouched by the Poles, as Pressac opines.[256] That is all Pressac has to say about this witness.

Pressac's general comment is as follows:[256]

"Whatever criticisms one might level at the accounts of these four witnesses, all affirm one identical fact: homicidal gassing took place in the morgue of Krematorium I. Even if their accounts diverge on the number of holes through which Zyclon-B was poured or on the number of extractors fans, details in fact unlikely to be noted and remembered unless one actually designed or installed them, the utilisation of the morgue for criminal purposes is established."

This conclusion is incredible: Pressac disregards the mandatory critical analysis of the testimonies for the evaluation of their credibility, he jettisons the obvious contradictions the testimonies contain, and limits himself to noting a generic agreement on an assumed fact, which actually demonstrates nothing. Such an agreement can also come about on the basis of completely unfounded rumors, such as the "steam chambers" of Treblinka, the "electrocution devices" of Belzec, or the "chlorine chambers" of So-

---

[254] J.-C. Pressac, *op. cit.* (note 33), p. 123.
[255] *Ibid.*, pp. 126f.
[256] *Ibid.*, p. 128.

bibór.[257] In the present case, as shown above, the concordance is a purely literary one. The witnesses having simply re-elaborated a literary story made up of pure propaganda in their accounts.

Pressac's conclusions are also at odds with the historiographical method which he claims he has used throughout his book *Auschwitz: Technique and Operation of the Gas Chambers* and which he falsely proclaimed to have newly introduced into the historiography about the Holocaust. This method is (ideally) based on documents and was to demonstrate "the complete bankruptcy" of the previous historiography on the Holocaust, as he defines it:[258]

"A history based for the most part on testimonies, assembled according to the mood of the moment, truncated to fit an arbitrary truth and sprinkled with a few German documents of uneven value and without any connection between them."

This definition fits perfectly well Pressac's own historical treatment of the alleged homicidal gassings in Crematorium I (but it also applies to the so-called "Bunkers" of Birkenau).

In his second book on Auschwitz, Pressac has tried to remedy this serious gap by presenting more ambitious arguments, seemingly based on documents. I shall deal with the latter in Chapter 5.

4.3. Franciszek Piper

If ignoring the two pages of introduction on the general history of the crematorium, the four pages which contain drawings and photographs, and the two pages of quotations from Rudolf Höss's and Pery Broad's accounts, Piper dedicated precious little space to the essential question of the homicidal gassings in the morgue of Crematorium I in his paper mentioned above. He reiterates Danuta Czech's assertions on the period of activity of the alleged gas chamber (September 1941 through early December 1942) and Filip Müller's statements on the number of victims (several tens of thousands). Yet, Piper supplies us with noteworthy new details. The first one is:[259]

"In view of the high temperature inside the building, the camp administration placed an order with the Boos firm for the installation of mechanical extrac-

---

[257] C. Mattogno, J. Graf, *Treblinka. Extermination Camp or Transit Camp?* Theses & Dissertations Press, Chicago 2004, pp. 47-62; C. Mattogno, *Belzec in Propaganda, Testimonies, Archeological Research, and History*, Theses & Dissertations Press, Chicago 2004, pp. 9-22; Jürgen Graf, Thomas Kues, Carlo Mattogno, Sobibór: Holocaust Propaganda and Reality, The Barnes Review, Washington, DC, 2010, pp. 71f.

[258] J.-C. Pressac, *op. cit.* (note 33), p. 264.

[259] W. Długoborski, F. Piper (eds.), *op. cit.* (note 35), Polish: p. 108; Engl. p. 128.

tion fans. These were installed in late February 1941, ventilating the furnace room, the morgue, and other rooms."

In a note, the Polish historian refers to Pressac's book *Les crématoires d'Auschwitz: La machinerie du meurtre en masse*, and adds:[260]

"Former prisoner Michal Kula was employed in the installations of the fans, APMO, Hoss Trial, vol. 25, pp. 17-18."

Piper continues:[259]

"After the 'experimental' killing by gas of several hundred Russian POWs and ill prisoners, the room previously used as morgue was rebuilt as a gas chamber. The doors leading to the lavatory and the furnace room were insulated, and several openings were made in the ceiling slab. Zyklon B was dropped in through these openings."

In a note, he says, *i.a.*:[261]

"The openings were made by the prisoner Czesław Sułkowski. APMO, Collection of Testimonies, vol. 74, p. 74. The openings were closed again when Crematorium I was converted into an air-raid shelter. Four openings were reconstructed after the war on the basis of visible traces; according to Broad and Müller, there were six openings."

The work by Boos concerns the installation of the first system of enhanced (but not mechanical)[262] ventilation, done towards the end of February 1941. In Chapter 5, I will examine Pressac's interpretation, from which F. Piper obtains his information.

Piper's reference to M. Kula's deposition is clearly misleading. Let us read, first of all, what the witness had to say:[263]

"In 1942, Höss became interested in the metal workshop, and particularly in the tools of the crime. Of course, he turned to us in the metal workshop. Ordered to do so by him, we fashioned various things: he supervised us personally. All the crematoria were partly constructed by the metal workshop. Only the equipment [i.e. the furnaces] came from the outside, but the anchoring bars of the furnaces, the grates, anything made of steel was done by the metal workshop. [...]

First there was the small crematorium in Auschwitz, for which a ventilator was made in our metal workshop. This ventilator was worked on by Maliszewski Stefan, Szablewski Stanisław, Stecisko Mieczysław, and by me. We worked until midnight. Before midnight, Höss came to see us, accompanied by Grabner. He made a big fuss, because the job was not yet done. It was about the ventilator for the aeration of the gas chamber; an opening had been made there, into

---

[260] *Ibid.*, Polish fn. 400.

[261] *Ibid.*, Polish fn. 402.

[262] Because it did not use ventilators; it worked by means of the chimney draft.

[263] Declaration by M. Kula of March 15, 1947. Höss trial, AGK, NTN, 107 (vol. 25), pp. 481f.

which the ventilator was set to draw out the gas. Before midnight we raced to the crematorium with the ventilator, screwed it in, and we were taken back to the camp by the SS. Along the road to the crematorium, we met some 300 persons who ran towards the crematorium."

A little earlier, Piper himself asserts of the alleged gassings in the homicidal gas chamber of the crematorium:[264]

"Former prisoner Michal Kula witnessed 300 POWs being herded into the crematorium."

This quotation brings us to September 1941, the month during which gassings of Soviet POWs are claimed to have started in the morgue of Crematorium I, but the temporary ventilation device was installed seven months earlier, at the end of February!

Furthermore, this ventilation system, as I have already explained, did not require a ventilator, because it worked thanks to the pressure difference generated by the draft of the crematorium chimney. Besides, Grabner's requisition of June 7, 1941, for the morgue of the crematorium concerned two fans, one for the air intake, one for the exhaust, not just one. But this requisition, for the simple reason of chronology, could have had nothing to do with the alleged homicidal gassings.

It follows that the ventilator mentioned by Kula could not have been used neither for the first nor for the second ventilation system, because Kula's account does not fit the facts. Hence Piper's interpretation is thus erroneous on two counts: technically and chronologically.

As for the ex-detainee Czesław Sułkowski, Piper refers to an account the Sułkowski gave on September 28, 1971, and in which he declared:[265]

"Earlier, we had built a furnace for the crematorium. I personally made the openings in the ceiling of the morgue where the first Soviet POWs were gassed. I saw those Russians while they were being taken there. They stood in the street, near the Blockführerstube between the present hotel and the crematorium, hundreds of them, all naked, and waited to be gassed. I saw the SS dumping the gas through the openings into the morgue."

Sułkowski worked in the camp as a bricklayer and was, therefore, a member of the bricklayer section of the Construction Office. The normal procedure was for the Construction Office to transmit to the appropriate section of the workshops a numbered order using a special form,[266] which described the work to be done and gave the exact dimensions and, where

[264] W. Długoborski, F. Piper (eds.), *op. cit.* (note 35), vol. III, Polish: p. 109, note 405; Engl.: S. 129, Fn. 405.
[265] APMO, Oświadczenia, vol. 74, pp. 6f.
[266] C. Mattogno, *The Central Construction Office of the Waffen-SS and Police Auschwitz. Organization, Responsibilities, Activities*, 2nd ed., Castle Hill Publishers, Uckfield 2015, pp. 50f. and Documents 40f. on pp. 123f.

needed, a sketch. In turn, the work shop section filled out a "labor card," which mentioned the object of the corresponding order with the dates for the beginning and the end of the work. On the back would be listed the consumption of materials.

If the detainee Sułkowski had actually opened up holes in the ceiling of the morgue, he would have had to follow the precise instructions of the corresponding order and of the "labor card," *i.e.*, in this particular case, the number, dimensions, and positions of the openings. But there is no trace of such documents.

Not only that, but he himself, who should have been able to clarify this controversial point of orthodox historiography, gave only a very terse account of the alleged work and was not even able to say how many openings he had personally installed.

Thus, his testimony is only of a very low value.

4.4. Robert Jan van Pelt

In his work on Auschwitz, over 500 pages long, Robert Jan van Pelt has made no historical analysis of the alleged homicidal gassings in Crematorium I. He limits himself to quoting – without any critical observation – the corresponding account by Pery Broad, presenting it as follows:[267]

> *"The Broad report, which was of independent origin, corroborated important elements of the picture that had begun to emerge in Sehn's investigation and added important new descriptions. Perhaps most important was Broad's recollection of the first gassings in Crematorium 1, which was located adjacent to his own office in the barrack that housed the camp's Political Department."*

As I have established in Chapter 3.6., Broad's "report" is completely unreliable. Van Pelt even claims that it describes "the first gassings in Crematorium 1," forgetting that Broad had stated that he witnessed *only one* homicidal gassing, which had taken place in July 1942, whereas the "first" gassings are said to have started in September 1941 according to van Pelt!

When he writes that the crematorium "was located adjacent to his own office housed in the camp's Political Department," van Pelt makes a mistake, because the barrack of the Political Department near the crematorium, designated "BW 86, interrogation barrack of Political Department (near crematorium)" was built between January 9 and 20, 1943,[268] and was

[267] R.J. van Pelt, *The Case for Auschwitz. Evidence from the Irving Trial.* Indiana University Press, Bloomington/Indianapolis 2002, p. 225.
[268] *Tätigkeitsbericht des SS-Ustuf. Kirschnek* for the period January 1 to March 31, 1943. RGVA, 502-1-26, p. 60.

handed over to the camp command on February 8, 1943,[269] hence at a time when the alleged gassings had officially ended. As we have seen above by means of Broad's statement, which is correct in this regard, the offices of the Political Department were at that time located on the ground floor of the SS infirmary.

Van Pelt had dealt briefly with the alleged gassing in Crematorium I in a previous book, written in collaboration with Deborah Dwork. After having discussed the difficulties the SS had run into with the first alleged gassing in Block 11, van Pelt gives a fictionalized account of the alleged first gassing in Crematorium I:[270]

> "*Fritzsch remembered that the morgue of the crematorium in the Stammlager had a flat roof; it would be a simple matter to make one or more openings in it. He also knew that, a month or so earlier, the morgue had been equipped with a new and powerful ventilation system. As we have seen, the Political Department had begun to use the morgue as an execution site for those convicted by the Gestapo Summary Court. From the beginning, the executioners had complained about the nauseating smell, because it also served as a morgue for the bodies of inmates who had died. Maximilian Grabner, the chief of the Political Department, had prevailed on Schlachter to install a more sophisticated ventilation system that not only extracted the foul air but also brought in fresh air from the outside. Fritzsch realized that such a ventilation system could deal with poisonous gas.*
> *Fritzsch's men punched three square portholes through the morgue roof and covered them with tightly fitting wooden lids. The number of 900 Soviets inaugurated the new gas chamber on September 16. 'The entire transport fit exactly in the room,' Höss recalled. 'The doors were closed and the gas poured in through the openings in the roof. How long the process lasted, I don't know, but for quite some time sounds could be heard. As the gas was thrown in some of them yelled: 'Gas' and a tremendous screaming and shoving started toward both doors, but the doors were able to withstand all the force.'*
> *A few hours later the fans were turned on and doors opened.*"[271]

Van Pelt claims that the morgue of Crematorium I had been transformed into a homicidal gas chamber immediately after the alleged first gassing in Block 11. He insinuates that SS-*Hauptsturmführer* Karl Fritzsch had had openings for the introduction of Zyklon B inserted in the flat roof of that room, but this is mere conjecture without any documentary foundation,

---

[269] Documentation concerning "transfer negotiation" (*Übergabeverhandlung*). RGVA502-2-150, pp. 7-9. Cf. my study on *The Central Construction Office, op. cit.* (note 266), Document 13, p. 78.
[270] D. Dwork, R. J. van Pelt, *Auschwitz 1270 to the Present*, W.W. Norton & Company, New York-London 1996, p. 293. The section of the book devoted to the history of KL Auschwitz was evidently written only by van Pelt.
[271] Editor's remark: van Pelt's translation of Höss's text is inaccurate and therefore different than the one quoted earlier (Chapter 3.5.). This will be discussed further below.

similar to the claim that the Political Department used the morgue for executions.

Van Pelt further affirms that "a month or so earlier, the morgue had been equipped with a new and powerful ventilation system," with reference to Grabner's letter of June 7, 1941. Actually, as we have seen in Chapter 2, nothing proves that Grabner's request had been fulfilled immediately. On the contrary, the documents say that the first work on the ventilation of Crematorium I after that date was carried out between the end of September and the middle of October 1941, hence after the alleged first gassing in Crematorium I.

The date of the "first gassing" adopted by van Pelt (September 16, 1941) is taken from Czech's *Kalendarium*, but I have shown in Chapter 4.1. that both the date and the alleged event have no documentary basis and are simply the fruit of the Polish authoress's deception.

The claim that "Fritzsch realized that such a ventilation system could deal with poisonous gas" is another arbitrary assertion without documentary basis, as is the assertion that follows:

> *"Fritzsch's men punched three square portholes through the morgue roof and covered them with tightly fitting wooden lids."*

Here, van Pelt's dilettantish superficiality exceeds all bounds: no document establishes a link between Fritzsch and the alleged openings for the Zyklon B. To be precise, no document at all speaks of their installation. Van Pelt takes his reference to the "three square portholes" from an essay by Pressac,[272] who, however, adduces as proof a photograph[273] from 1945! On the other hand, as for the "wooden lids," van Pelt simply relied on the Polish "reconstruction" of 1946–1947!

Höss's testimony, as is clear from the critical analysis I have presented in Chapter 3.5., is absolutely unacceptable, hence completely devoid of historical value. It is also at variance with van Pelt's own thesis, because the Auschwitz commandant affirms that the openings for the Zyklon B were being cut "through the layer of earth and the concrete that constituted the roof of the morgue" while the transport of 900 Soviet POWs was being unloaded, something which Pressac rightly considers highly "unlikely." Therefore, van Pelt had to omit the corresponding passage in Höss's declarations.

Van Pelt's final sentence – "A few hours later the fans were turned on and doors opened" – is a real masterpiece of deception, aiming at underpinning surreptitiously the presence of a "powerful ventilation system" in the morgue that permitted a homicidal gassing without the inconveniences

[272] J.-C. Pressac, R.J. van Pelt, *op. cit.* (note 43), p. 209.
[273] *Ibid.*, note 64 on p. 243. I shall deal with this question in detail in Chapter 6.

of Block 11. Why should it ever have been necessary to wait "a few hours" before opening the doors in the first place? There is no reason.

Van Pelt says so only because Höss wrote: "It was only several hours later that [the room] was opened and aired out." By changing the meaning of this sentence, van Pelt wants to establish, underhandedly, an equivalence between Höss's "*entlüftet*" (aired out), which, as we have seen, clearly refers to a natural ventilation, and "the fans," thus creating an imaginary "convergence of proof."

Chapter 5:
Pressac in 1993 on Homicidal Gassings
in Crematorium I

5.1. The Projects for Ventilation Systems in Crematorium I

In this section we will examine how Jean-Claude Pressac interpreted the documents relating to ventilation systems in Crematorium I. He wrote:[274]

"As Topf had not yet submitted a modified proposal for the ventilation of the crematorium, Schlachter turned to the Friedrich Boos Co. at Bickendorf near Cologne to have a temporary ventilation device installed for the transitional period until the final equipment could be installed by Topf. Boos, at the time, was building a central heating system in the barracks of the SS guards. The company was the only civilian firm then operating within the camp with both the necessary know-how and the material needed for the installation. This unit was installed between February 23 and March 1. No technical data are known, but SS-Rottenführer Pery Broad of the Political Department did leave us a description of what it looked like on the outside: '(...) the fat angled metal tube (...) that stuck out from the roof (of the crematorium) and was monotonously humming. (...), that this was the exhaust fan which was supposed to render the air in the morgue breathable, at least to some extent.'"

A few pages further on, Pressac returned to the argument:[275]

"When both furnaces were in operation – and that was now the case nearly every day – the heat became so great that now hot air would come into the morgue from the furnace hall when the ventilation was switched on – the very opposite of what was desired. In order to prevent this from happening, the ventilation flaps of the morgue had to be shut, with the result that there was no longer any ventilation. With the summer heat it now became almost impossible to spend any time there, for the air was filled with dangerous vapors, and flies as well as other sources of disease were drawn. Grabner reported this 'scandal' to the Construction Office, asking 'in the general interest' for ventilations to be installed in the morgue, with one fan for aeration and a second one, in

---

[274] J.-C. Pressac, *op. cit.* (note 34), p. 18. Cf. J.-C. Pressac, R.J. van Pelt *op. cit.* (note 43), p. 193.
[275] J.-C. Pressac, *op. cit.* (note 34), p. 23. Cf. J.-C. Pressac, R.J. van Pelt *op. cit.* (note 43), p. 197.

suction, for ventilation. The exhaust air was to be fed into the chimney of the furnaces (a solution that had already been considered).

This sinister episode has a great significance. It proves that Grabner, by making use of his rank and by the fear which his section caused among the subordinates in the Construction Office, became involved in the affairs of Crematorium I. It documents that in the morgue – because it was ventilated mechanically – killings by means of poisonous gas could take place. This becomes apparent for the first time here, because it was being planned not only to drawn out stale air from a morgue, but also to blow in fresh air."

Finally, Pressac states:[276]

"the crematorium disposed of a mechanical ventilation which – as long as it was used exclusively for the ventilation of the morgue – was sufficiently powerful."

The source for the installation of the ventilation given by Pressac is the weekly report of head of construction Schlachter, mentioned in Chapter 2.

It is erroneous to assume – as I have already explained – that this ventilation was mechanical. That it was put in by the Boos Co. is, on the other hand, a mere assumption by Pressac, unsupported by any evidence.

The quotation from Pery Broad, which Pressac introduces to explain how the ventilation operated, is distorted and truncated: according to the witness, the suction ventilator (exhauster) was not for the furnace hall *and* the morgue, but only for the morgue, because the exhaust fan was supposed "to render the air in the morgue breathable, at least to some extent,"[277] something rather obvious, inasmuch as in the furnace room the fresh air feed was made possible by a window[278] with bars. As we can see, Pressac – while admitting that the technical details of this device are "not known" – thinks he knows them better than Pery Broad, to the point of being able to "correct" him.

Furthermore, Pressac truncates the quotation, leaving out the conclusion of Pery Broad's description: that on the roof of the morgue "there were – in addition to the exhaust fan – six air-holes with lids."[279] The reason for that omission is clear: it is too blatantly at variance with Pressac's assertion that in January 1942 "three rectangular openings were cut into the ceiling of the morgue and equipped in such a way that *the Zyklon B could be introduced*" (my italics).[276] I will return to this question in Chapter 6. Here, let it only be

---

[276] J.-C. Pressac, *op. cit.* (note 34), p. 34. Cf. J.-C. Pressac, R.J. van Pelt *op. cit.* (note 43), p. 209.

[277] Pery Broad, *op. cit.* (note 200), p. 19.

[278] *Ibid.*, p. 20.

[279] *Ibid.* In the French translation used by Pressac this term is rendered as *"orifices d'aérage"* (aeration openings). *Auschwitz vu par les SS*, Edition du Musée d'Etat à Oświęcim, 1974, p. 166.

said that to open up "six aeration holes" in a room having an exhaust fan does not make much sense.

Moreover, Pressac commits a serious methodical error: He claims to explain a situation existing at the end of February 1941 with an account referring to a point in time after May 1942. As we have seen above, Pery Broad was transferred to Auschwitz on April 8, 1942,[280] and assigned to the Political Department on June 18. Yet the structure of the crematorium as Broad describes it cannot be dated earlier than it stood in June 1942, because it is known that the yard of the crematorium was fenced in and equipped with an entry and an exit gate no earlier than the end of May. Hence, the description given by this witness is later by at least 15 months than February 1941.

The drawing referred to by Pressac – drawing no. 1434 of July 3, 1942 – confirms Pery Broad's account merely with respect to the "angled metal tube" visible on the roof of the crematorium, but the function Pressac ascribes to it in the legend of the drawing squarely contradicts Pery Broad's statement, because it is said to be "the angled *air exhaust* (furnace and corpse room) installed by the Friedrich Boos Co. of Köln-Bickendorf"[281] (my italics). As if by magic a fresh-air feed suddenly becomes an exhaust tube.

Pressac understood moreover little or nothing about the malfunctioning of the ventilation system mentioned by Grabner in his letter to the SS *Neubauleitung* of June 7, 1941, which we have already examined in Chapter 2: the warm air did not enter the morgue "from the furnace room," as Pressac affirms, but from the flue of the furnaces, which is very clear, because this ventilation was connected to the "discharge channel," *i.e.*, precisely to the flue, and it is likewise obvious that the exhaust air from the morgue reached the chimney along with the smoke from the furnaces. Thus, in this respect, too, Pressac misunderstood Grabner's request: Grabner did not request that "the air taken in should then be conveyed to the chimney of the furnaces," because this was already being done and was the very cause of the inconvenience. He wanted the exhaust air to be taken to the chimney by a *special duct* and not by means of the flue. Aside from this, Grabner wanted *two* fans – one for fresh-air intake, one for exhaust – simply because, hitherto, there had been *none at all*. Otherwise he would have requested only *one* ventilator for the fresh-air feed.

The ventilation system set up in the morgue at the end of February 1941 was thus artificial, but not mechanical (unless operated by means of the chimney's forced draft device). It worked in an artificial way on the basis of the chimney's draft (the low pressure in the flue sucked in the air from

---

[280] *Sterbebücher von Auschwitz, op. cit.* (note 94), vol. I, "Täterbiografien", S. 271.
[281] J.-C. Pressac, *op. cit.* (note 34), explanations of Document 8 outside of the text.

the morgue, which was directly connected to it), but for the flue to be connected to the morgue, one certainly did not need a company like Boos; ordinary bricklayers supervised by the Topf specialist who had just finished the installation of the second furnace could have done the job.

Pressac says that this inconvenience has "great significance," and he insists that it revealed an explicit homicidal willingness, as "becomes apparent for the first time here, because it was being planned not only to drawn out stale air from a morgue, but also to blow in fresh air." This only shows, however, that Pressac knows next to nothing about ventilation technology.

In actual fact, if any ventilation is to function at all, a fresh air feed is indispensable, as otherwise there would be no air exchange. Thus, the first proposal for a ventilation of the morgues submitted by Topf and specifying 20 exchanges of air per hour insisted that "a source of fresh air has to be provided for the morgues by means of windows or other openings."[282]

It is thus clear that the only novelty in Grabner's request was that he wanted a mechanical ventilation. From what has been said it becomes evident that the ventilation installed in the morgue at the end of February 1941 could function only as long as the room also had an air intake. Where did this air come from? If we exclude the two doors and the walls,[283] there is only the ceiling, which should have had aeration openings in addition to any alleged openings for the introduction of Zyklon B.

It is certainly true that thanks to such a ventilation "killings by means of poisonous gas could take place," but during the ventilation it would have been necessary to leave the aeration and/or Zyklon B feed apertures open, which is exactly the opposite of what is said in the testimony of witnesses on the alleged homicidal gassings.

Finally, when he says that Grabner used his function and the terror it inspired to meddle in the affairs of the crematorium, Pressac makes another serious mistake.[284] Actually, the Political Department of the camp also functioned as a morgue police unit, thereby supervising by law the cremation of the bodies of detainees who had died[285] and their registration in the death records[286] (*Sterbebücher*) kept for this purpose. In keeping with the rules in force for civil morgue practices, the Political Department also

---

[282] Letter of Topf to *SS-Neubauleitung* dated December 9, 1940. RGVA, 502-1-312, p. 136.

[283] The two outside walls were covered by the earth embankment which surrounded the building; as for the two internal walls, one separated the morgue from the furnace hall, the other separated it from the room later labeled "*Waschraum*," (corpse) washing-room.

[284] As we have seen above, van Pelt has taken over this imbecile idea, writing that Grabner "had prevailed on Schlachter."

[285] Legislation in force specified that cremations had to be authorized by the local police, who also kept a register of all cremations. F. Schumacher, *Die Feuerbestattung*, J. M. Gebhardt's Verlag, Leipzig 1938, pp. 118f.; *Reichsgesetzblatt*, 1938, part I, pp. 1000f.

[286] W. Długoborski, F. Piper (eds.), *op. cit.* (note 35), vol. I, Polish: pp. 122-134; Engl.: pp. 180-184.

oversaw the treatment of the ashes of those cremated, which explains the frequent requests for urns from the SS-*Neubauleitung.*[287]

5.2. The "First Gassing" and the Wearing Out of the 2nd Furnace

If we follow Pressac, the "first homicidal gassing" at Auschwitz took place between "December 5 [1941] and the end of the month."[276] Referring to it, the author explained:[276]

> *"The victims, whose number is somewhere between 550 and 850, were cremated in the two double-muffle furnaces of the crematorium over a period of one to two weeks of intensive work. This caused damage to the second furnace."*

Pressac's source is the "letter of SS-man Grabner of January 31, 1942."[288] The text quoted immediately above reads as if Grabner had written that the corpses of those allegedly gassed had been cremated in the furnaces at a rate that had eventually damaged furnace no. 2. But Grabner actually said in this very brief letter merely:[289]

> *"As a Topf & Söhne engineer is presently in this camp for the installation of a furnace, maintenance is requested on furnace no. 2 in the local crematorium, which is in need of repair."*

Hence, there is no connection between the damage on furnace no. 2 and the claimed cremation of the victims of the alleged gassing. Pressac's conjecture is furthermore invalidated by the fact that his date for the "first gassing" is arbitrary in every respect and is based on a critical observation of mine demonstrating that Czech's official interpretation is false![290] In this regard, Dwork and van Pelt explicitly declare that "Pressac's dating of the first gassing in December 1941 is not substantiated by evidence"[291] – but this is true for *any* dating of the gassing.

Examining the documents shows how artificial Pressac's interpretation really is. In December 1941, preparations for the installation of the third furnace were under way in the crematorium. The Topf & Söhne specialist Mähr worked in the crematorium from November 27 to December 4, pouring the foundation for the third furnace and repairing one of the other two,[292] and that is why Pressac takes December 5 to be the beginning of the

---

[287] The first request of this kind known to me is *"Anforderung Nr. 33"* of February 5, 1941, for *"100 Stück Urnenkisten"* (100 pcs. urn boxes). The request is from: *"Politische Abteilung/Krematorium."* RGVA, 502-2-1, p. 46.

[288] J.-C. Pressac, *op. cit.* (note 34), note 21 on p. 113.

[289] RGVA, 502-1-312, p. 77.

[290] C. Mattogno, *op. cit.* (note 1), p. 159; cf. *op. cit.* (note 2), p. 8.

[291] D. Dwork, R. J. van Pelt, *op. cit.* (note 270), note 46 on p. 412.

[292] RGVA, 502-1-312, p. 82; APMO, BW 11/1, pp. 4f.

period, during which the gassing is claimed to have taken place. But a specialist from Topf – probably Mähr himself – was also present in the crematorium between December 18 and 26, 1941.[293] Hence the period during which the cremation of the claimed gassing victims may have taken place is reduced even further.

Ironically, the reality of the alleged "first gassing" is based exclusively on testimony, but none of these accounts states explicitly that it took place in December 1941, which is why Dwork and van Pelt reject Pressac's thesis.

5.3. The Alleged Homicidal Gassings in Crematorium I

On the subject of the homicidal gassings in Crematorium I, Pressac asserted:[276]

> *"Three rectangular openings were made in the ceiling of the morgue and equipped in such a way that Zyklon B could be introduced. It was poured directly into the room, in which the two doors had previously been made gastight. The roar of the engine of a truck parked next to the crematorium drowned out the screams of the agonizing victims.*
>
> *The SS was able to carry out gassings there between January 1942 and the resumption of work on the third furnace in May, i.e., over a period of four months. Today it is assumed that only relatively few gassings with poison gas were done in this crematorium, but that their frequency has been exaggerated because they made a deep impression on the direct or indirect witnesses."*

Pressac, in fact, believed that "the third double-muffle furnace was assembled in May and delivered at the end of that month,"[294] and justified his assertion as follows:[295]

> *"The dates are not indicated, but are certain due to the following facts:*
> *1) Arrival date of the rail-car containing more steel parts for the third furnace (contract No. 41 D 1980): April 30, 1942 (ZAM, 502-1-313)*
> *2) Posting date, May 8, 1942, of first reminder sent by Topf (ZAM, 502-1-327), out of a total of eight, to activate payment for the third furnace (the down payment had been made on January 31, 1941)*
> *3) Normal installation time for a double-muffle furnace: 15 days, drying time not included (1 month altogether)*

---

[293] RGVA, 502-1-312, p. 82.
[294] J.-C. Pressac, *op. cit.* (note 34), p. 38. Cf. J.-C. Pressac, R.J. van Pelt *op. cit.* (note 43), p. 210. Here, however, the translation is wrong: "Only the iron fittings for the third double-muffle furnace were of immediate use."
[295] J.-C. Pressac, *op. cit.* (note 34), note 120 on p. 102.

4) Report by SS-man Pollock of May 30, 1942, on damage to the chimney of Crematorium I that had occurred due to overheating (ZAM, 502-1-312 and 313)"

The dates indicated by Pressac are so "certain" that on April 10, 1942, detainee No. 20,033, the Polish engineer Stefan Swiszczowski, who worked in the Central Construction Office as a draftsman,[296] drew an "Inventory map of building Nr. 47a, BW 11 crematorium," in which the third furnace is already present.[297] This furnace was actually built in March 1942, and work had ended by the 31st of that month, as evidenced by the building schedule plan for March 1942, which lists 100% completion of the addition to the crematorium as of March 31.[298] This date is also confirmed by the report on the state of construction dated April 1, 1942.[299] Pressac's error is serious, but his explanation is even more so, because it shows a rather superficial reading of the documents, to say the least.

Let us start with item 1). The parts of the third furnace, including reinforcing steel, were shipped by Topf on October 21, 1941, as part of Central Construction Office order no. 41/1980/1, and arrived at Auschwitz on October 27.[300] It is true that on April 16, 1942, some elements of anchor bolts for a double-muffle furnace covered by order No. 41/1980/1[301] were loaded into a rail-car containing "parts for the triple-muffle furnaces," which was destined for the future Crematorium II of Birkenau, as per Central Construction Office order No. 41/2249/1. These anchor bolt, however, did not belong to the third furnace at Auschwitz, as Pressac believes, but were for Mauthausen, and were shipped to that camp on September 22,[302] as is indisputable from a comparison of the list of these parts[303] with the Topf

---

[296] RGVA, 502-1-256, p. 171.
[297] *"Bestandsplan des Gebäudes Nr. 47a B.W.11. Krematorium."* Drawing No. 1241 of April 10, 1942. 502-2-146, p. 21. Cf. Document 4.
[298] *Baufristenplan* of April 15, 1942. RGVA, 502-1-22, p. 11.
[299] *"Baubericht über den Stand der Bauarbeiten"* of April 15, 1942. RGVA, 502-1-24, p. 320.
[300] Topf, *Versandanzeige* (shipping advice) of October 21, 1941, shipment in car no. 43225 Munich (G). RGVA, 502-1-312, pp. 104f.
[301] Topf, *Versandanzeige* of April 16, 1942. RGVA, 502-1-318, pp. 167-170. The car arrived at Auschwitz not on April 30, but on April 18. Pressac confuses the date at the end of the document – which refers to the verification of the goods in the car against the *Versandanzeige* and to the receiving of these goods by the Department of Materials, as attested by the stamp *"Materialverwaltung Richtigkeit bescheinigt"* – with the arrival date of the car, which was certified by a stamp on the first page of *Versandanzeige* and was initialed by the *Bauleiter*.
[302] Letter from Central Construction Office to Mauthausen camp of September 30, 1942. RGVA, 502-1-280, p. 273.
[303] *Aufstellung* (list) of ZBL of September 26, 1942. BAK, NS4 Ma/54.

shipment list of April 16, 1942. Pressac himself mentions this shipping error[304] but does not understand its significance.

As for item 2), the reminder sent by Topf on May 8 has no relation whatsoever with the installation of the third furnace. Not only did Pressac fail to wonder why Topf should have reshipped parts for anchoring the furnace which had already been shipped, he also failed to consider why this reshipment did not appear on any of Topf's invoices. Actually, Topf's partial invoice for the third furnace, dated December 16, 1941, and approved by Bischoff on December 22, amounted to 7,518.10 Reichsmark.[305] Based on this invoice, the Central Construction Office authorized a payment order of 3,650 RM on January 7, 1942, in partial payment, which was paid on January 27.[306] Topf sent a second partial invoice, likewise backdated to December 16, 1941, which arrived at Auschwitz on May 22, 1942,[307] for a remainder of 3,868.10 (*i.e.* the difference between the cost estimate of 7,518.10 RM and the sum of 3,650 RM already paid by the SS administration). The final invoice, also backdated to December 16, 1941, arrived at Auschwitz on July 10, 1942, and amounted to 3,786.10 RM – 82 RM less for a rotating disk[308] which had been deducted from the previous partial invoice because the item had not been delivered.[309] The payment order for the final payment of this amount was authorized by the Central Construction Office on July 17, 1942, and payment went out on July 29.[310]

Item 3) contains accurate information, but Pressac uses it erroneously, because the drying-out of the furnace was not done in May 1942, but in March.

Finally, item 4) is in all respects irrelevant. SS-*Oberscharführer* Josef Pollock's report of May 30, 1942,[311] refers exclusively to the crematorium chimney and does not even mention the number of furnaces in existence.

This said, let us go on to the alleged homicidal gassings in the Auschwitz crematorium starting at "January 1942." Between January 14 and 21,

---

[304] J.-C. Pressac, *op. cit.* (note 34), p. 52. Cf. J.-C. Pressac, R.J. van Pelt *op. cit.* (note 43), p. 218.
[305] Topf, *Rechnung* no. 2363 of December 16, 1941. 502-2-23, p. 263-262a.
[306] *Abschlagszahlung* (down payment) no. 1 for J.A Topf & Söhne in Erfurt of January 7, 1942. 502-2-23, pp. 262-262a. Pressac erroneously gives the date January 31 as mentioned in Topf's *Schlussrechnung* (final invoice), which however refers to the day the bank draft no. Z 8005314 issued by the treasury department (*Amtskasse II*) of HHB on January 27 was cashed (by Topf).
[307] Topf. *Teil-Rechnung* dated December 16, 1941. 502-1-327, pp. 114-114a.
[308] The rotating disk was a replacement for the rails on which the "coffin introduction carts" ran in the furnace hall of Crematorium I.
[309] Topf, *Schlussrechnung* dated December 16, 1941. 502-1-23, pp. 261-261a.
[310] ZBL, "*Schlussabrechnung über Lieferung und Errichtung eines Einäscherungsofens der Firma J.A. Topf & Söhne,*" Erfurt, July 17, 1942. (Final account of supply and installation of a cremation furnace) 502-2-23, pp. 258-259a.
[311] RGVA, 502-1-312, p. 64 and 502-1-314, p. 12.

the inmate metal workshop of the Central Construction Office carried out the repair of three "furnace doors"[312] and of two furnace grills.[313]

On January 16, the same shop received an order for "redrilling of anchor holes for furnace-anchoring" and to "fabricate a frame 50 x 50 according to instructions by fitter." The job was done between January 22 and 24.[314] On January 31, as we have already seen, a Topf specialist was certainly present at Auschwitz, who was undoubtedly the "fitter" mentioned above and who therefore worked at the crematorium at least from January 16 onwards,[315] if not earlier. The repair of the second furnace requested by Grabner was carried out on February 4, as is shown by a handwritten note on his previously mentioned letter.[289]

On February 10, the inmate metal workshop worked on the repair of "2 doors for the fire place" and made "4 pcs. angle irons,"[316] which were part of the anchoring structure of the furnaces. It is therefore highly likely that the Topf specialist remained on site at least until that date in order to do the repairs that were needed.

As we have already seen earlier, the third furnace was installed in March. Likewise, on May 14 and 15 there was work in the engine room, and the flue linking the furnaces to the chimney was repaired. During the second half of May, external work was done on the crematorium: the yard in front of the crematorium was fenced in and equipped with two wooden gates, and the old pavement was replaced.

Toward the end of the month, the metal brace of the chimney became loose, and there was a danger of collapse. It became necessary to demolish and rebuild the chimney.

Plainly, there remained precious little time for any homicidal gassings without them being witnessed by many outsiders!

If we assume the reality of gassings, the behavior of the Auschwitz authorities with regard to the ventilation equipment becomes decidedly senseless. What is more, in Pressac's attempt at an explanation, he makes matters even more unreasonable.

---

[312] The term may refer indiscriminately to the doors of the muffles (*Einführungstüren*), or to the ash removal traps (*Ascheentnahmetüren*) or to the doors of the hearths (*Feuertüren*).

[313] *Häftlingsschlosserei*, *Arbeitskarte* of January 13, 1941, Auftrag Nr. 630. RGVA, 502-2-1, p. 71.

[314] *Häftlingsschlosserei*, *Arbeitskarte* of January 16, 1942, Auftrag. Nr. 651. RGVA, 502-2-1, p. 60.

[315] Pressac asserts that the "engineer" mentioned in Grabner's letter was Kurt Prüfer (J.-C. Pressac, *op. cit.* (note 34), p. 35), but the only source of this information is Grabner's letter! (*Ibid.*, note 113 on p. 101). Pressac has deduced Prüfer's presence – not documented anywhere – from the misspelled title "Ingineur" contained in that letter. Actually, Grabner has only conferred an unsuitable designation to the Topf fitter who was working in the crematorium.

[316] *Häftlingsschlosserei*, *Arbeitskarte* of February 3, 1942, Auftrag Nr.747. RGVA, 502-2-1, p. 61.

On March 15, 1941, SS-*Neubauleitung* ordered the ventilation system proposed by Topf as per the company's cost estimate dated February 24, *i.e.*, two weeks after the installation of the temporary ventilation hook-up in the morgue. The latter, therefore, was only an unsatisfactory stop-gap measure for a normal morgue, for the alleged homicidal gassings are said not to have actually started until six months later. Topf shipped the definitive equipment at the end of 1941, but there is no documentary evidence that it was ever installed. The invoice of May 27, 1943, in fact, is only for 1,884 RM for the delivered equipment itself, but does not include the 596 RM for installation.

In September 1941, we are told, the alleged homicidal gassings started in Crematorium I with a temporary makeshift ventilation system. In July 1942, with the demolition of the old chimney, this ventilation stopped functioning as well, but it occurred to no one to install the Topf ventilation equipment in the crematorium, which was rusting away in a warehouse. This happened only on November 27, 1942, on the eve of the cessation of the alleged homicidal gassings in Crematorium I, when Central Construction Office suddenly put ventilation back on the agenda. Its installation was declared urgent on November 30:

> *"The fitter you offered can start <u>immediately</u> with the installation of the ventilation system in the <u>old</u> crematorium at Auschwitz concentration camp."*

Pressac had his own way of explaining this oddity in his reference to Bischoff's letter of November 30, 1942:[317]

> *"The sequence of jobs laid out for Prüfer clearly shows the intent to kill, which the SS was harboring at the time: the gassings were to take place in 'Leichenkeller 1' of Crematorium II as soon as it became available. If, however, there should be a delay in the arrival or the equipment ordered, it was necessary to be able to fall back on the morgue of Crematorium I, provided it possessed the definitive ventilation. This equipment had already been supplied and had a capacity of 8,300 m³ of air per hour, with 3,000 m³ per hour for the morgue itself. The latter fact was decisive, even though it entailed the disadvantage that the gassings had to be moved back to the Main Camp, where anyone could witness them. This was exactly the opposite of the original plan, that is to say, to move them to Birkenau, away from the Main Camp."*

But a few pages earlier, Pressac had written:[318]

> *"Because for each gassing the area around the crematorium had to be cordoned off with considerable disturbance for the everyday operation of the camp, and because [gassings] were completely impossible whenever civilian workers were active on the site, it was decided, at the end of April, to move the gassings to Birkenau."*

[317] J.-C. Pressac, *op. cit.* (note 34), 61.
[318] *Ibid.*, p. 35. Cf. J.-C. Pressac, R.J. van Pelt *op. cit.* (note 43), p. 209.

But if the alleged gassings had been transferred to the so-called bunkers at the end of April 1942 for the express reason that the SS wanted to keep them away from the detainees and the civilian workers, and because they wouldn't disrupt the camp's daily routine there, and if they had been conducted there without a hitch for seven months, why should the SS bring them back to the Main Camp at the end of November of that year?

Pressac's hypothesis is absolutely unreasonable. In this context, it is also quite unclear why the SS should have continued homicidal gassings in Crematorium I up to the end of April 1942, if they had set up "Bunker 1" for this purpose, which is said to have gone into service on March 20.

As for the ventilation equipment, which the SS – Pressac claims – wanted to set up in Crematorium I for their homicidal gassings, Pressac makes a serious mistake. If we disregard the fact that the capacity of the fan was 8,600 and not 8,300 m^3 of air per hour, his claim that 3,000 m^3 were for the morgue has no foundation.

As we have already seen, the cost estimate of December 9, 1940, was based on 10 exchanges of air per hour for the dissecting room and 20 for the morgue. The system was to work with a single fan, no. 450, driven by a motor of 1.5 HP for 6000 m^3 of air per hour. The difference in the number of exchanges between the two rooms was due to the diameter of the corresponding ducts, smaller for the dissecting room, larger for the morgue.

The cost estimate of February 3, 1941, has the same specifications for dissecting room and morgue, but includes a separate ventilation for the furnace room, consisting of a fan (no. 300), driven by a motor of 0.75 HP to deliver 3,000 m^3 of air per hour.

The cost estimate of February 24 was for a single ventilator for the dissecting room, morgue, and furnace room. The fan was more powerful – no. 550 – and driven by a correspondingly more powerful motor, 3 HP, for 8,600 m^3 of air per hour. Of the total volume, 3,000 m^3 per hour were assigned to the furnace room, and the remaining 5,600 to the dissecting room and morgue.

The reduction of 400 m^3 per hour for the total throughput in the two earlier estimates (6,000 m^3 per hour) is easily explained: the third estimate took into account a modification of the morgue, done some months before, in which an urn storage room had been walled off.[319] The morgue lost that part of the room located behind the second furnace of the crematorium, thereby diminishing the volume of air to be extracted. In practice, the partial capacity of the installation set aside for the dissecting room and morgue remained unchanged – 10 changes of air for the former, and 20

---

[319] The creation of the *Urnenraum* was announced to Topf by Bischoff in a letter dated January 21, 1941. RGVA, 502-1-327, p. 185.

changes for the latter – or, in terms of air volume, some 4,500 m³ per hour for the morgue and 1,100 m³ per hour for the dissecting room.

Chapter 6:
The Openings for the Introduction of Zyklon B:
Material Evidence

6.1. The Modifications of Crematorium I (1944–1947)

Drawing no. 1241 of Crematorium I, dated April 10, 1942, shows a morgue (17.60×4.60 m), a "washing room" (4.17×4.60 m) and a "laying-out room" (4.10×4.60 m).[320]

According to orthodox historiography, the morgue was transformed into a homicidal gas chamber from September 1941 on by fitting it with two gas-tight doors and breaking through its roof an uncertain number of openings for the introduction of Zyklon B. The number of openings testified to was, in fact, one for Rudolf Höss (session of March 12, 1947, of his trial), two for Stanisław Jankowski and for Hans Stark, three for Jean-Claude Pressac, four for the Soviet commission of investigation, and six for Pery Broad and Filip Müller. Last but not least, the worker who allegedly made these openings – the detainee Czesław Sułkowski – who should have been the person best informed about their number, their dimensions, their shape, their structure, and their location – as we have seen in Chapter 4.3 – mentioned nothing about their number or features.

If we follow drawing No. 4287, dated September 21, 1944 (see Document 5), the transformation of the crematorium into an air-raid shelter involved splitting up the morgue into four rooms by means of three partitions. In the first room, on the south side, an air lock of 2 m by 2 m was set up with a door to the outside. Furthermore, the vestibule, which lay behind the main entrance to the crematorium, obtained a partition wall, and the other walls were strengthened, resulting in another air lock (3.87×3.45 m).

According to the letter from Josten already mentioned, "7 pcs. doors gas-tight and fragment-proof"[321] had been foreseen, but Jothann's cost estimate of November 2, 1944, mentions "6 pcs. simple interior doors."[322] Actually, for reasons of economy, the camp administration had apparently only three "gas-tight and fragment-proof" doors installed – those of the two air locks (still existing) and the one leading into the furnace room, which

---

[320] RGVA, 502-2-146, p. 21. Cf. Document 4.
[321] RGVA, 502-1-401, p. 34.
[322] RGVA, 502-2-147, p. 12a.

until the end of 1993 was leaning against one of the walls of that room. It had probably been removed by the Germans themselves when they changed the layout of the air-raid shelter at some point in 1944 by walling up the door leading into the former furnace room. The six partitions were merely equipped with ordinary doors, the two small toilet stalls received two doors 70 × 200 cm, as is shown in plan no. 4287 and from Josten's letter of August 26, 1944: "2 pcs. single doors 70 by 200 cm."[323]

But then what happened to the two alleged gas-tight doors of the alleged homicidal gas-chamber? One of them – the one which separated the morgue from the furnace hall – is said to have been dismantled and temporarily replaced by a standard gas-tight air-raid shelter door like the two outer doors. The other, which separated the washing room from the laying-out room, was simply removed and substituted by an ordinary door. The present door even has a glass window, see. Document 34.

Needless to say, at the liberation of the camp not the slightest trace of the two gas-tight doors of the alleged homicidal gas chamber were found, and not a trace of them exists in the documentation of the Central Construction Office.

Between 1946 and 1947, in an effort to "reconstitute" the "original state" of the alleged homicidal gas chamber, the Poles demolished not only the three partitions mentioned above, but also the one that separated the original morgue from the washing room. In the space thus obtained, they made four openings in the roof – the alleged openings for the introduction of Zyklon B – into which they inserted small wooden casings with lids (see Documents 23-25).

Today, therefore, the alleged gas chamber of Crematorium I is 21.32 m long, *i.e.*, 4.32 m longer than the original room. The Poles also created an opening in the wall linking the morgue with the furnace room (the original one had been walled up by the SS at some point in 1944), but moved it half a meter out of its original position and gave it a rather crude, unsymmetrical shape.

6.2. The Alleged Openings for the Introduction of Zyklon B

6.2.1. Jean-Claude Pressac's Interpretation

In 1989, J.-C. Pressac published one photograph from a series taken by Stanisław Luczko, probably in May 1945 (see doc. 18). It shows the flat roof of Crematorium I.[324] The French historian gave it the title "Dance on the roof of the old crematorium" and commented on it as follows:[324]

---

[323] RGVA, 502-1-401, p. 34.
[324] APMO, sygn. 5149; J.-C. Pressac, *op. cit.* (note 33), p. 149.

"View of the roof of Krematorium I, looking south-north, 1945 (May?). The chimney has not yet been rebuilt. The features of the roof are:
– two ventilation chimneys for the furnace room (two-tone with a dark cap)
– two other brick chimneys, probably for ventilating the air raid shelter in view of their newly-built appearance
– in addition, on a line parallel to – and to the left of – that on which the two brick chimneys are built, it is possible to see THREE places where the former traps for introducing Zyklon-B have been filled in, thus indicating that the morgue had been used as a gas chamber.
Above the stage, dominated by a red star with the hammer and sickle, fly the flags of Poland (left) and the Soviet Union (right), with lamps mounted above them.
This photograph proves that a dance was organized in 1945 on the roof of Krematorium I, and that people actually danced above the homicidal gas chamber. This episode appears almost unbelievable and sadly regrettable, and the motives for it are not known. This photo also proves that the present covering of roofing felt and the zinc surround of the roof are not original."

Hence, Pressac undertakes to demonstrate the 1941 creation of three openings in the ceiling of the morgue on the basis of a photograph taken in 1945. Let us look into this question more closely.

The ex-detainee Adam Żłobnicki made the following declaration in a statement given on November 18, 1981:[325]

"I remember perfectly well that the openings for the introduction of Zyklon B, which were located on the flat roof of this crematorium, were also remade.[326] The reconstruction was made easier by the fact that at the locations of the former insertion openings there remained clear traces after the sealing of the former openings with cement. At these very points, the openings were re-established and the little chimneys[327] built with bricks. This work, too, was done in 1946–1947."

The four shafts reconstructed by the Poles are arranged as shown in my drawing (see Document 17). They are grouped in two parallel pairs along the internal (A-B) and the external (C-D) walls of the morgue. Shafts C and D are 82 cm from the outer wall, shaft A is 90 cm and shaft B 85 cm from the inner wall. Shafts A-B are 6.30 m and shafts C and D 8.30 m apart from each other respectively. The four shafts thus form the vertices of an irregular parallelogram having a height of 2.40 meters.

What is interesting here is that in the present state of the room shaft D stands 5.10 m from the wall with the entrance from the outside, shaft C stands 7.10 m from the opposite wall which separated the washing room

---

[325] APMO, Oświadczenia, t. 96, p. 59.
[326] Earlier, the narrator had spoken of the reconstruction of the chimney of Crematorium I that was carried out between late 1946 and early 1947.
[327] The small wooden casings set in the ceiling panels of the morgue.

from the laying-out room, shaft B stands 7.10 m from the wall of the little vestibule near the entrance and shaft A stands 5.10 m from the opposite wall. Such an arrangement makes sense only within the framework of the *present* state of the morgue. It is, in fact, clear that the position of the shafts was based on their distance from the short, transverse walls of the present room by rationally subdividing the available distance of some 21.3 meters: thus shafts A and D were placed at 5.10 m, shafts B and C at 7.10 m from the nearest wall.

The distance for shaft B was, curiously, not based on the rear wall, but on the partition of the little vestibule, and this caused shaft B to be moved back by 2 m with respect to shaft D. But at the time of the alleged original layout of the morgue's shafts, the little vestibule did not exist, whereas there was at that time a partition between the washing room and the morgue. Thus, this arrangement of the shafts makes sense only for the present state of the crematorium and therefore cannot be original.

If we consider the *original* layout of the morgue (see Document 15), the arrangement of the shafts strikes us as most irrational, because while shaft D would still be 5.10 m from the rear wall, shaft B would now be 9.10 m from it, shaft A 0.7 m from the partition of the washing room and shaft C some 2.8 m from the last. The irrationality of this arrangement becomes all the more apparent if we realize that, as a result, one half of the morgue near the washing room ($8.5 \times 4.60 = 39.1$ m^2) would have been equipped with three shafts (A, B, and C), whereas the other half of equal area would have had only one – shaft D!

Let us now look at the 1945 photograph published by Pressac. The three dark spots (designated 1, 2, and 3 in Document 18) are aligned parallel to the two brick ventilation chimneys, the first one of which (the one closest to the camera) is located on top of the morgue. Furthermore, the first dark spot appears to the right of the first chimney (S2 in Documents 16 and 17), whereas in the reconstruction by the Auschwitz Museum the alleged opening for the introduction of Zyklon B closest to this ventilation chimney ("B," see Documents 15-17) is to its left. If these dark spots were the traces of the alleged Zyklon B introduction openings and if, as the witness Żłobnicki tells us, the present openings were located where the traces of the original openings appeared, why was no opening made at the point where dark spot no. 1 can be seen? Inversely, the Auschwitz Museum had an opening made (point "C" in docs. 15-17) at a point where the photograph in question shows no dark spot.

When the crematorium was transformed into an air-raid shelter for the SS infirmary, the work sheet indicated:[328]

> *"Creation of ducts and wall openings for the heating furnaces and the ventilation intake and outlet."*

and, more specifically:

> *"5 pcs. wall openings for devices."*

Today the walls surrounding the morgue show no traces of former openings. What is more, the outside wall was and still is covered by an earth embankment, as is the rear wall as well, with the exception of the narrow passage through this embankment leading to the entrance door. On the other hand, the front wall is completely bare and has only one window on the side of the morgue. Finally, the wall between the morgue and the furnace hall shows no traces of openings either, and it would have made no sense, anyway, to pierce it for the installation of stove pipes or ventilators.

Thus it is clear that the five openings mentioned above were created in the ceiling of the rooms that had been turned into an air-raid shelter.

In the ceiling of the morgue, in its present state, there are two rectangular ventilation shafts, one in a corner of the former laying-out room (the later surgery room, marked as S1 in Documents 16 and 17), the other in a corner of the second air-raid shelter room seen from the entrance (S2). Due to their location right at the wall, it is generally assumed that these shafts were added during the transformation of the building into an air-raid shelter.

In addition to these two shafts, one can still distinguish the traces of four *circular* openings that have been crudely walled in.[329] They originally had a diameter of about 35 cm. The corresponding traces are situated (as measured from their centers) at 1 m, 7.2 m, 8.5, and 18.30 m from the rear wall of the morgue (where the entrance is today), and at distances of 1.0 m and 1.4 m from the wall between the morgue and the furnace hall (see Documents 15-17, 19-22).

Because the original morgue was 17 m long, the fourth opening is located in the ceiling of the room in which the corpses were washed until 1943 (the washing room). That is the first proof that those openings had nothing to do with the alleged Zyklon B introduction devices. The second proof is their shape – circular instead of square.

---

[328] *"Kostenüberschlag zum Ausbau des alten Krematoriums als Luftschutzbunker für SS-Revier mit einem Operationsraum im K.L. Auschwitz O/S – BW 98 M."* RGVA, 502-2-147, p. 126.

[329] The left-most room in docs. 15-17, which originally served as a laying-out chamber and in which today the Kori oil-fired furnace from the crematorium at Trzebinia is preserved, is not open to tourists. I have therefore been unable to ascertain whether its ceiling shows traces of any further openings.

We therefore have six original openings in the ceiling of the rooms under investigation, four of which have been walled up at some point. The document mentioned above, however, refers only to five openings to be added.

From other documents it can be deduced that there must have been a ventilation opening in the ceiling of the morgue when it was actually used to store corpses.[330] It can be assumed that opening no. 1 was this ventilation opening, first of all because intelligent design suggests putting a ventilation opening at one end of a long room, and second because the area around opening 1 turned into a vestibule on the building's transformation into an air-raid shelter, for which a ventilation opening was not required.

6.2.2. The Interpretation by the Holocaust History Project

Three members of the Internet-based Holocaust History Project – Daniel Keren, Jamie McCarthy, and Harry W. Mazal – have considered the photograph published by Pressac with the aim to "correct some common misconceptions about the Crematorium I gas chamber, specifically about the location of the Zyklon holes."[331]

The authors affirm that there were originally five holes for the introduction of the Zyklon B in the roof of the crematorium, a figure which is at odds with all the testimonies. Thus, depending on the witnesses and the historians, the number of openings present at the same time was either 1, 2, 3, 4, 5 or 6!

On the photograph in question, they identify the traces of a fourth dark spot in the roofing felt on the roof of the crematorium (see Document 18, spot no. 4.), which had obviously escaped J.-C. Pressac's attention. They then state that four of the alleged five holes for the introduction of Zyklon B, which the Poles had made in the post-war years, were sunk exactly where the aforementioned dark spots were located, and labelled them Z3 [= 3 in my Document 18], Z2 [= 2] and Z4 [= 4]; dark spot Z1 [= 1] was not reopened, according to the authors, whereas dark spot Z5, which they place between Z3 and Z2, does, in fact, not appear on the photograph.

The authors claim to have identified the traces of an alleged opening Z1 on the ceiling of the morgue, and provide a photograph of it.[332] What we are dealing with here are traces of the opening that I have designated #2 which, however, was not square, as the authors claim, but round, and was

---

[330] RGVA, 502-1-327, pp. 191f., 502-1-312, p. 111.
[331] D. Keren, J. McCarthy, H.W. Mazal, "The Ruins of the Gas Chambers: A Forensic Investigation of Crematoriums at Auschwitz I and Auschwitz-Birkenau," in: *Holocaust and Genocide Studies,* vol. 9, n. 1, spring 2004, pp. 97-99.
[332] *Ibid.,* figure 31 on p. 92.

actually not at the location of Z1 but 2 m from it toward shaft B (see Documents 15-17, 21).

In any case, the authors themselves deny that the traces of openings #3 and #4 correspond to the dark spots in the photograph published by J.-C. Pressac, because the former have a round shape:[333]

> "*At two other locations holes were sealed, but these were circular ventilation openings.*"

Dark spot Z1 was located practically on the perpendicular of dark spot Z4, as results from the extension of the respective sides (see Document 18), and was thus on the prolongation of the axis A-B in front of the present opening D (see Documents 15-17). In this area there is no trace of any walled-up opening in the ceiling of the morgue.

Hence, no opening in the roof of the morgue – current or former – corresponds to dark spot Z1. But then, why should dark spots Z2, Z3, and Z4 correspond to openings? As a matter of fact, spot Z2 is too far away from ventilation shaft S2 to be identical with today's shaft "B," and spot Z3 is too close to ventilation shaft S1 – probably located over the washing room – to be identical with today's shaft "A." Spot Z4, on the other hand, appears to be too far away from the wall to be identical with today's shaft "D," which is only 82 cm away from the wall.

The authors claim that, when the crematorium was converted into an air-raid shelter, the alleged Zyklon B introduction openings were sealed again,[334] but this assertion, which they owe to Franciszek Piper,[335] has no documentary basis and is disproved by the cost estimate of November 2, 1944, mentioned above, which not only does not speak of any kind of closing up of existing holes, but specifies the creation of five openings in walls, *i.e.* in the ceiling, as I have pointed out above. If there would have been holes already in the roof, the SS would have used those instead of further weakening the roof – which was, after all, meant to protect from bombs – by adding more holes.

The authors furthermore speak of the chemical proof:[336]

> "*As at the other gassing installations in the camp, cyanide compounds can still be detected in the chamber's walls, as forensic examinations by the Cracow Institute for Forensic Research demonstrate.*"

They refer here to an article by Jan Markiewicz, Wojciech Gubała, and Jerzy Łabędź.[337] Of the seven brickwork samples taken in the alleged gas

---

[333] *Ibid.*, p. 98.
[334] *Ibid.*, p. 97.
[335] F. Piper, *op. cit.* (note 36), p. 177, note 16: "When Crematorium I was converted into an air-raid shelter, the openings were bricked up."
[336] D. Keren et al, *op. cit.* (note 331), p. 97.

chamber (numbers 16-22), three gave negative results (samples 18, 19, and 21), the others showed a maximum content of 292 micrograms (0.292 milligrams) of cyanides per kilogram of material.[338]

Leaving aside the strange decision by the Polish scientists to exclude Iron Blue (Prussian Blue) from the cyanide compounds to be detected by chemical analysis (which explains the extremely low values they found, as compared to the samples taken by Germar Rudolf and Fred Leuchter), another point on which the Polish chemists can be taken to task is that they did not indicate exactly where they took their samples.

Fred Leuchter has done this. The plan of Crematorium I in appendix III of his report[339] shows the locations in the present morgue, from which he took his 7 samples. One of them, sample no. 28, contained 1.3 milligrams (1,300 micrograms) per kilogram of substance, a value of the same order of magnitude as the other samples, except for one of them.[340] As opposed, however, to those samples which were taken in the space which originally belonged to the morgue, sample no. 28 – as has already been pointed out by Enrique Aynat[341] – was taken by Leuchter from the wall separating the washing room from the laying-out room, which was not part of the original morgue and thus not part of the alleged gas chamber.

Therefore, the presence of cyanides in sample no. 28 cannot be explained by homicidal gassings, only either by normal disinfestations or by a limit of the detection method.[342] But then, why should it not be possible to explain the other traces of cyanide in the morgue in the same innocuous way?

6.3. Conclusion

The four openings now on the roof of the morgue are not original, and the dark spots which appear on the photograph published by J.-C. Pressac were not traces of openings (as borne out by the fact that the location of no for-

---

[337] Jan Markiewicz, Wojciech Gubała, Jerzy Łabędź, "A Study of the Cyanide Compounds Content in the Walls of the Gas Chambers in the former Auschwitz and Birkenau Concentration Camps," *Z Zagadnień Nauk Sądowych* (Problems of Forensic Sciences), vol. XXX, 1994, pp. 17-27.

[338] *Ibid.*, Table III on p. 23.

[339] Fred A. Leuchter, *An Engineering Report on the Alleged Execution Gas Chambers at Auschwitz, Birkenau and Majdanek, Poland*, Samisdat Publishers, Toronto 1988; more recent: F.A. Leuchter et al., *op. cit.* (note 181), pp. 59, 61.

[340] In order, the values are as follows: 1.9 – 1.3 – 1.4 – 1.3 – 7.9 – 1.1 mg/kg.

[341] E. Aynat, "Neither Trace nor Proof: The Seven Auschwitz 'Gassing' Sites According to Jean-Claude Pressac," *Journal of Historical Review* 11(2) (1991), pp. 177-206, here p. 182.

[342] See. G. Rudolf, *op. cit.* (note 181), pp. 243f.

mer or current opening in the ceiling corresponds to that of any of these dark spots).

Furthermore, sealing any openings in the roof of the crematorium would hardly have left dark spots of such clarity. To level the surface of an opening that has been filled with cement mortar, a simple wooden board larger than the hole itself is enough; but if one had wanted to create such clear dark spots, it would have been necessary to painstakingly scratch out the cement on the surface of the hole filled with mortar. It would have amounted to a form of sabotage on the part of the bricklayer unit to leave such obvious traces of the alleged openings. No detainee would have risked that because on the inside, on the ceiling of the morgue, obvious traces of the closure of the holes would have remained apparent anyway.

The detainees of the roofing detail would have had to perform a similar kind of sabotage by shaping the roofing felt to fit exactly the profile of the alleged quadrangular depressions in the cement.

The explanation of the dark spots is much simpler: they were caused by compression of the roofing felt, which had become soft from sunlight, under the weight of a flat and heavy object, such as a cement vase or other decoration for the Soviet-Polish dance frolic. That explains why the fold in the roofing felt is so marked along the edges, instead of being slightly concave.

The photograph published by Pressac demonstrates that, in the spring of 1945, the Soviets and the Poles believed so strongly in the story of the homicidal gas chamber in Crematorium I that they thought nothing of organizing a ball and dancing on its roof!

Chapter 7:
Summary and Conclusion

1) There is no proof that the alleged openings for the introduction of Zyklon B ever existed in the morgue of Crematorium I.
2) There is no proof that the morgue was ever equipped with two gas-tight doors.
3) In contradiction to any kind of logical planning, these alleged gas-chamber doors are said to have later been removed by the SS, when the crematorium was converted to a *gas-tight* air-raid shelter, and replaced by one normal door and one standard gas-tight door.
4) The traces of cyanides present in the walls of the morgue do not prove that the room was used as a homicidal gas chamber.
5) The number of openings made by the Poles after the war (four) is at variance with all available testimonies. This also goes for the figure adopted by the members of the Holocaust History Project (five).
6) The Polish "reconstruction" of both the location of the openings and the structure and dimensions of the Zyklon B introduction shafts has no basis in documents or in witness statements. In fact, there are no documents, and no witness has furnished any detailed information on these.
7) There is no proof that the four dark spots visible on the roof of Crematorium I in the photograph published by Pressac are traces of former openings that were later sealed; on the contrary, the location of no former hole in the morgue's ceiling corresponds to the location of any of these dark spots.
8) The remaining traces of former openings in the ceiling are circular and are no doubt connected to the transformation of the crematorium into an air-raid shelter.
9) The openings created by the Poles make sense, geometrically speaking, only in the context of the present state of the room, but are totally asymmetric and irrational when seen in the context of its original state – which is further proof that they have nothing whatsoever to do with any alleged original openings.

The story of homicidal gassings in the morgue of Crematorium I attracted no particular interest from the various underground resistance groups at

Auschwitz. They used it only once in their propaganda reports, and rather late at that.

The testimonies on alleged gassings are meager and mutually contradictory. The most detailed ones, and thus those that can be checked most easily, are notoriously and demonstrably false. In this category we find primarily the accounts by Filip Müller and Pery Broad. Notoriously and demonstrably false is also the claim about the only alleged homicidal gassing for which we have verifiable data (date, number, nationality, origin, and serial numbers of the victims): the gassing of the so-called "*Sonderkommando*" of December 1942.

The "reconstructions" by the orthodox historians are purely conjectural and fictitious. Having no documentary basis, they rely entirely on "accounts collected at the spur of the moment, adjusted to produce arbitrary truths," according to the well-known practice, which Pressac ascribes to all previous historiography, but which applies to him as well.

An examination of the archives of *Neubauleitung* (later *Bauleitung* and finally *Zentralbauleitung*, Central Construction Office) of Auschwitz allows us to retrace the history of the ventilation projects for the crematorium elaborated by the Topf firm, and to establish with sufficient precision how the various temporary systems installed there were set up and how they worked. These projects and their realizations were carried out in line with the needs of a normal morgue and not a "homicidal gas chamber" as hypothesized without the least documentary evidence.

Finally, an analysis of the alleged Zyklon B introduction openings in the roof of the morgue demonstrates that the openings installed by the Poles in the immediate post-war period are necessarily in keeping with the architectural structure at that time, which was different from the structure the crematorium had in 1942. For this reason, they cannot have any relationship with the alleged original openings. In any case, there is no material or documentary trace of the latter.

The alleged use of the morgue of Crematorium I at Auschwitz as a gas chamber has therefore no historical foundation. It is not history but historical propaganda, laboriously reworked over the decades.

Appendix

Documents

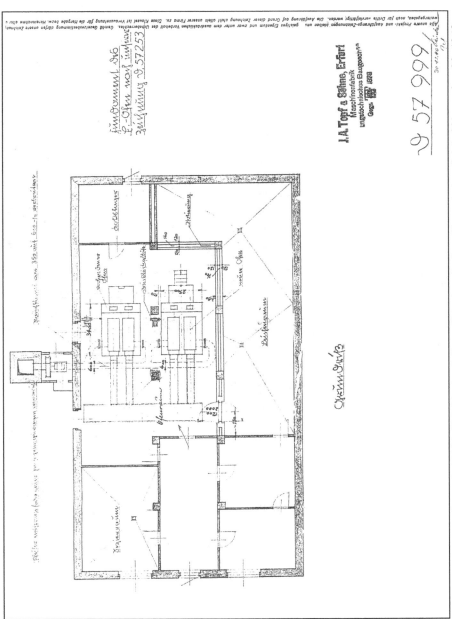

Document 1: Topf plan D 57999, "SS-Neubauleitung, K.L. Auschwitz – Krematorium," dated November 30, 1940. RGVA, 502-1-312, p. 135.

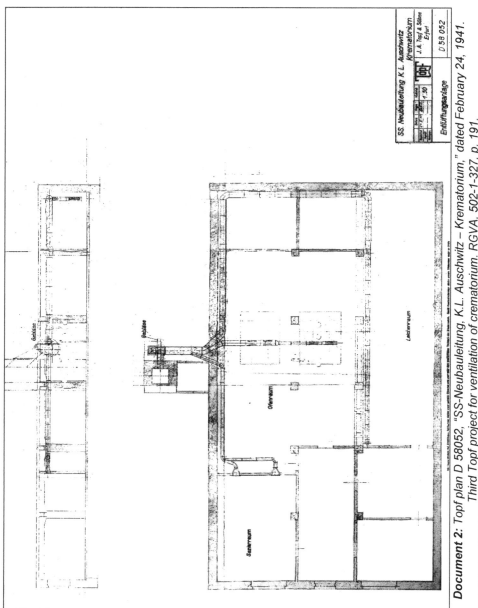

Document 2: *Topf plan D 58052, "SS-Neubauleitung, K.L. Auschwitz – Krematorium," dated February 24, 1941. Third Topf project for ventilation of crematorium. RGVA, 502-1-327, p. 191.*

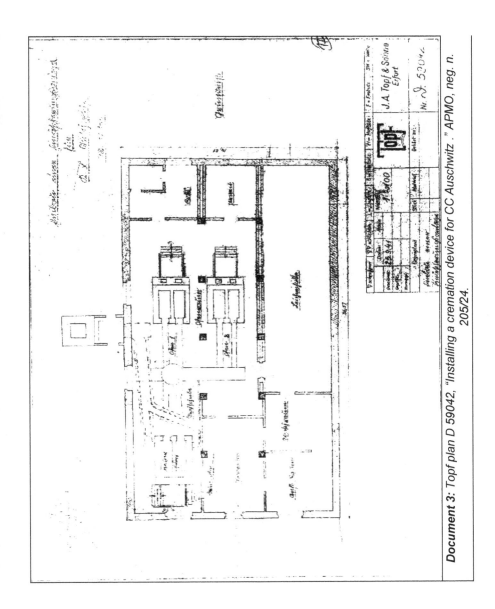

Document 3: *Topf plan D 59042, "Installing a cremation device for CC Auschwitz ." APMO, neg. n. 205/24.*

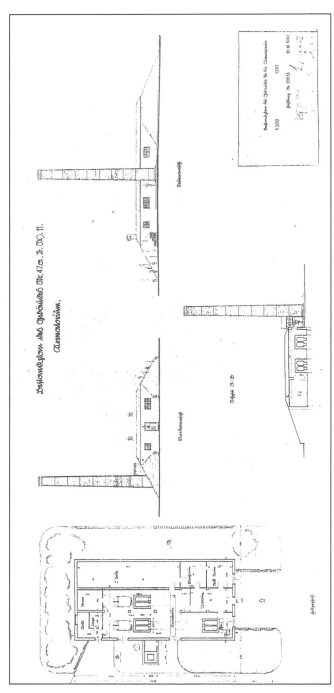

Document 4: *Inventory plan of Building No. 47a. B.W. 11. Crematorium. Plan No. 1241, dated April 10, 1942. RGVA, 502-2-146, p. 21.*

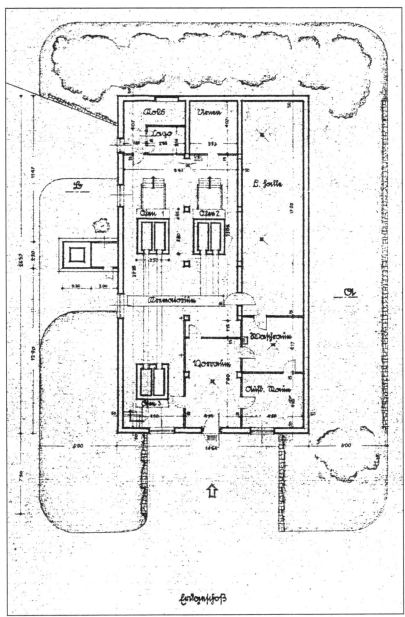

Document 4a: *Section enlargement of Document 4.*

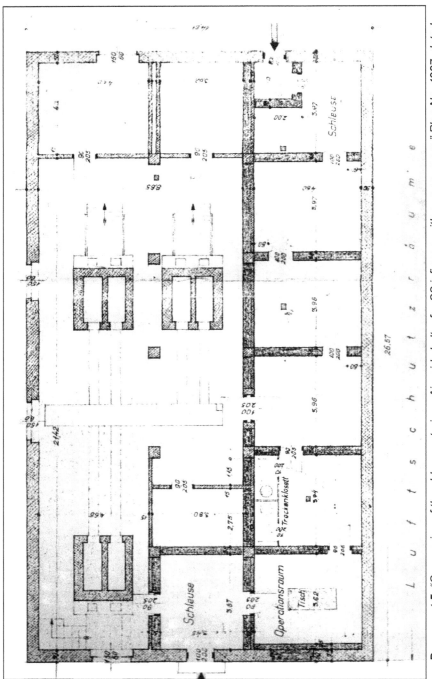

Document 5: *"Conversion of the old crematorium. Air-raid shelter for SS infirmary with surgery room." Plan No. 4287, dated September 21, 1944. RGVA, 502-2-147, p. 20.*

J. A. TOPF & SÖHNE

MASCHINENFABRIK UND FEUERUNGSTECHNISCHES BAUGESCHÄFT

60 JAHRE

ERFURT
POSTFACH 552/₈
FABRIK UND VERWALTUNG
DREYSESTRASSE 7/₉

DRAHTWORT
TOPFWERKE ERFURT

FERNRUF
251 25 251 26 251 27 251 28

UNSER ARBEITSGEBIET:
    Entwurf und Ausführung
    vollständiger Kesselhäuser
    Verbesserungen u. Umbauten
    bei nicht wirtschaftlicher
    Dampferzeugung

Abteilung D I
    Wärmewirtschaftliche Unter-
    suchungen und fachmännische
    Beratung
    Wärmebilanzen
    Eigen-Herstellung und Liefe-
    rung sämtlicher wärmetechn.
    Anlagen, Apparate und Vor-
    richtungen
Topf-Spezial-Feuerungen für
    alle Brennstoffe: Steinkohle,
    Braunkohle, Schwelkoks, Torf,
    Sägespäne, Holz usw.
Vollmechanische Topf-Roste
Halbmech. Topf-Feuerungen
Topf-Wurfbeschicker „Ballist"
Topf-Spezial-Roststäbe
    Feuerungsarmaturen
Ölfeuerungen für sämtliche
    industrielle Betriebe
Vorwärmer, Lufterhitzer,
Dampfüberhitzer, Flugasche-
Ausblase-Vorrichtungen
Zugverstärkungsanlagen
Einmauerungen von Dampf-
    kesseln von industriellen Feue-
    rungen bis zu den größten
    Abmessungen usw.
Industrie-Schornsteinbau bis zu
    den größten Abmessungen
    Schmiedeeiserne Schornsteine
Industrie-Ofenbau zur Abfallver-
    nichtung, Müllverbrennung,
    Kabelverwertung, Vercrackung
Feuerbestattungs-Einrich-
    tungen mit moderner elek-
    trischer- oder Gas-Beheizung

Abteilung D II
    Sämtliche Transport-Anlagen
    Mechanische Bekohlung und
    Entaschung

Abteilung D III
    Lüftungstechnische Anlagen
    für industrielle Betriebe, Bade-
    anstalten, Gaststätten usw.
    Absaugeanlagen für Staub,
    Späne usw.
    Klimaanlagen
    Ventilatorenbau

Abteilung E III
    Pneumatische Förderanlagen
    für Kohle, Asche, Chemikalien,
    Getreide und alle luftförm-
    igen Schüttgüter

Abteilung C
    Eisenkonstruktionen und Be-
    hälterbau

Form 680 6. 38. 2000 G.

Kosten-Anschlag

UNSERE ABTEILUNG:
D III/Schu.

ANGEBOT Nr.
40/1096

HAUSAPPARAT Nr.
110

DATUM:
9.12.1940.

An den

Reichsführer SS
Chef der deutschen Polizei
Hauptamt Haushalt und Bauten
SS-Neubauleitung Auschwitz.

A u s c h w i t z / O.S.

Betrifft: Entlüftungs-Anlage für Leichenzellen

und Sezierraum.

Aufgestellt   Schu/fa

Geprüft

    Die Spezialfabrik für feuerungstechnische Anlagen TOPF
        hat Zehntausende von TOPF-Feuerungen geliefert.
        Hervorragende sechzigjährige Spezialerfahrungen.
    Eigene Versuchsstation und feuerungstechnisches Laboratorium.
    Untersuchung von Brennstoffen, Asche, Speisewasser.
                Eigene Lehrheizer.

Document 6: *Cost estimate by Topf dated December 9, 1940, for "ventilation system for morgue cells and dissecting room." RGVA, 502-1-312, pp. 138-140.*

J. A. TOPF & SÖHNE   2. Blatt des Kostenanschlages vom 9.12.1940.
    ERFURT
      [Topf]   für Auschwitz.

Lfd. Nr.	Anzahl	Gegenstand der Veranschlagung		
		Entlüftungs-Anlage für Leichenzellen und Sezierraum.		
1.	1	Gebläse Nr. 450 zur Förderung von stündlich 6000 cbm Abluft gegen eine Gesamtpressung von 25 mm WS bei einer Umdrehungszahl des Schaufelrades von 720/min und einem Kraftbedarf, an der Welle gemessen, von 1,1 PS.		
		Das Gebläse besteht aus einem schmiedeeisernen Gehäuse, einem Schaufelrad, welches fliegend auf Motorwellen-Stumpf aufgebaut wird, und einem Motorständer.		
		Preis RM		175,--
2.	1	Drehstrom-Motor für 220/380 Volt, 50 Perioden, mit Doppelnutanker für geräuscharmen Lauf, für eine Leistung von ca. 1,5 PS bei n = 720/min mit freien Wellende.		
		Preis RM		220,--
3.	1	Sterndreieckschalter, eingekapselt, mit Sicherungs-Element, jedoch ohne Sicherungen.		
		Preis RM		25,--
4.	1	Abluftrohr-Leitung, führend vom Sezierraum bis zum Gebläse in der Leichenzelle, 180 bis 450 mm Durchmesser ansteigend, einschließlich der Abzweiger, Rohrkrümmer, Rohr-Befestigungs- und Rohr-Verbindungen.		
		Preis RM		924,--
5.		Montage der Anlage, wofür wir einen Monteur nach dort entsenden. In den Kosten der Montage sind enthalten die Löhne, Verpflegungsgelder für den Monteur, sowie das leihweise Überlassen für die für die Monteure notwendigen Werkzeuge während der Dauer der Montage.		
		Preis RM		440,--
		RM		1.784,--

68. 1. 40. 8000. Cr.

Document 6 continued.

J. A. TOPF & SOHNE
ERFURT

[TOPF]

5. Blatt des Kostenanschlages vom 9.12.40.

für   Auschwitz.

Lfd. Nr.	Anzahl	Gegenstand der Veranschlagung	602	/	9/2
		Die Preise verstehen sich ab unserem Werk Erfurt ohne Verpackung. Letztere berechnen wir zu Selbstkosten und nehmen diese nicht zurück.			
		Lieferungsbedingungen A. 60.6.40.1000.			

68. 1. 40. 8000. Cr.

Document 6 continued.

54/11

J. A. TOPF & SÖHNE

MASCHINENFABRIK UND FEUERUNGSTECHNISCHES BAUGESCHÄFT

60 JAHRE

GEGR. [Topf] 1878

ERFURT
POSTFACH 552/₆
FABRIK UND VERWALTUNG
DREYSESTRASSE 7/₉

DRAHTWORT
TOPFWERKE ERFURT

FERNRUF
251 25 20126 25127 251 28

UNSER ARBEITSGEBIET:
Entwurf und Ausführung
vollständiger Kesselhäuser
Verbesserungen u. Umbauten
bei nicht wirtschaftlicher
Dampferzeugung

Abteilung D I
Wärmewirtschaftliche Unter-
suchungen und fachmännische
Beratung
Wärmebilanzen
Eigen-Herstellung und Liefe-
rung sämtlicher wärmetechn.
Anlagen, Apparate und Vor-
richtungen
Topf-Spezial-Feuerungen für
alle Brennstoffe: Steinkohle,
Braunkohle, Schwelkoks, Torf,
Sägespäne, Holz usw.
Vollmechanische Topf-Roste
Halbmech. Topf-Feuerungen
Topf-Wurfbeschicker „Ballist"
Topf-Spezial-Roststäbe
Feuerungsarmaturen
Ölfeuerungen für sämtliche
industrielle Betriebe
Vorwärmer, Lufterhitzer,
Dampfüberhitzer, Flugasche-
Ausblase-Vorrichtungen
Zugverstärkungsanlagen
Einmauerungen von Dampf-
kesseln von industriellen Feue-
rungen bis zu den größten
Abmessungen usw.
Industrie-Schornsteinbau bis zu
den größten Abmessungen
Schmiedeeiserne Schornsteine
Industrie-Ofenbau zur Abfallver-
nichtung, Müllverbrennung,
Kabelverwertung, Verzackung
Feuerbestattungs-Einrich-
tungen mit moderner elek-
trischer- oder Gas-Beheizung

Abteilung D II
Sämtliche Transport-Anlagen
Mechanische Bekohlung und
Entaschung

Abteilung D III
Lüftungstechnische Anlagen
für industrielle Betriebe Bade-
anstalten, Gaststätten usw.
Absaugeanlagen für Staub,
Späne usw
Klimaanlagen
Ventilatorenbau

Abteilung E III
Pneumatische Förderanlagen
für Kohle, Asche, Chemikalien,
Getreide und alle luftförder-
fähigen Schüttgüter

Abteilung C
Eisenkonstruktionen und Be-
hälterbau

Form. 88 a. B. 39. 2000 Cr.

UNSERE ABTEILUNG:
D III/Schu.

ANGEBOT Nr.
41/117

HAUSAPPARAT Nr.
110

DATUM:
3.2.1941.

Kosten-Anschlag

An den

Reichsführer SS
Chef der deutschen Polizei
Hauptamt Haushalt und Bauten
SS-Neubauleitung Auschwitz

A u s c h w i t z / O.S.

Betrifft   1 Entlüftungs-Anlage für Leichen- und
Sezier-Raum,

1 Entlüftungs-Anlage für Ofen-Raum.

Aufgestellt: Schu/fa.

Geprüft:

Die Spezialfabrik für feuerungstechnische Anlagen TOPF
hat Zehntausende von TOPF-Feuerungen geliefert.
Hervorragende dreißigjährige Spezialerfahrungen.
Eigene Versuchsstation und feuerungstechnisches Laboratorium.
Untersuchung von Brennstoffen, Asche, Speisewasser.
Eigene Lehrhäuser.

Document 7: *Cost estimate by Topf for "1 ventilation device for morgue and dissect-ing room, 1 ventilation device for furnace room," dated February 3, 1941. RGVA, 502-1-312, pp. 123-126.*

J. A. TOPF & SÖHNE　　　　2.　Blatt des Kostenanschlages vom　3.2.1941.
　　ERFURT
　　　[Topf]　　　für　Auschwitz.

Lfd. Nr.	Anzahl	Gegenstand der Veranschlagung			

A.　**Entlüftungs-Anlage für Leichenzellen-**
　　　　und Sezier-Raum:

1.　1　Gebläse Nr. 450 zur Förderung von
stündlich 6000 cbm Abluft gegen eine
Gesamtpressung von 25 mm WS bei einer
Umdrehungszahl des Schaufelrades von
720/min und einem Kraftbedarf, an
der Welle gemessen, von 1,1 PS.

Das Gebläse besteht aus einem schmie-
deeisernen Gehäuse, einem Schaufel-
rad, welches fliegend auf Motorwel-
lenstumpf aufgebaut wird, und einem
Motorständer.
Preis　　　　　　　　　　RM　　　　175,--

2.　1　Drehstrom-Motor für 220/380 Volt,
50 Perioden, mit Doppelnutanker für
geräuscharmen Lauf, für eine Lei-
stung von etwa 1,5 PS bei n = 720/
min. mit freiem Wellenende.
Preis　　　　　　　　　　RM　　　　220,--

3.　1　Sterndreieck-Schalter, gußgekapselt,
mit Sicherungs-Element, jedoch ohne
Sicherungen.
Preis　　　　　　　　　　RM　　　　25,--

4.　1　Abluftrohr-Leitung, führend vom Sezierraum bis zum Gebläse in der Lei-
chenzelle, 180 bis 450 mm Durchmes-
ser ansteigend, einschließlich der
Abzweige, Rohrkrümmer, Rohr-Befesti-
gungs- und Rohr-Verbindungen.
Preis　　　　　　　　　　RM　　　　867,--

5.　　Montage der Anlage, wofür wir einen
Monteur nach dort entsenden. In
den Kosten der Montage sind enthalten die Löhne, Verpflegungsgelder
für den Monteur, sowie das leihweise
Überlassen der für die Monteure not-
wendigen Werkzeuge während der
Dauer der Montage.
Preis　　　　　　　　　　RM　　　　440,--

Gesamtpreis Pos. A 1-5　　　RM　　　1.727,--

08. 9. 42. 10000. L. 0804 (3828)

Document 7 continued.

J. A. TOPF & SOHNE   3. Blatt des Kostenanschlages vom 3.2.1941.
   ERFURT
      [TOPF]   für   Auschwitz.

Lfd. Nr.	Anzahl	Gegenstand der Veranschlagung		
B.		Entlüftungs-Anlage für Ofen-Raum:		
1.	1	Gebläse Nr. 300 zur Förderung von stündlich 3000 cbm Abluft gegen eine Gesamtpressung von 15 mm WS bei einer Umdrehungszahl des Schaufelrades von 900/min und einem Kraftbedarf, an der Welle gemessen, von 0,6 PS.		
		Das Gebläse besteht aus einem schmiedeeisernen Gehäuse, einem Schaufelrad, welches fliegend auf Motorwellen-Stumpf aufgebaut wird, und einem Motorständer.		
		Preis RM		125,--
2.	1	Drehstrom-Motor für 220/380 Volt, 50 Perioden, mit Doppelnutanker für geräuscharmen Lauf, für eine Leistung von ca. 0,75 PS bei n = 900/min.		
		Preis RM		123,--
3.	1	Sterndreieck-Schalter, gußgekapselt, mit Sicherungs-Element, jedoch ohne Sicherungen.		
		Preis RM		16,--
4.	1	Abluftrohr-Leitung, führend von Mitte Ofenraum bis zum Gebläse, 225 bis 300 mm Durchmesser ansteigend, einschließlich der Rohrkrümmer, Rohr- Befestigungen, Ansaugegitter und Rohr-Verbindungen.		
		Preis RM		240,--
5.	1	Druckstutzen zur Verbindung der Ausblase-Öffnung des Gebläses mit dem gemauerten Abluft-Kanal.		
		Preis RM		42,--
6.	1	schmiedeeisernes Konsol, hergestellt aus kräftigem Profileisen, für die erhöhte Aufstellung des Gebläses.		
		Preis RM		42,--
7.		Montage der Anlage, wofür wir einen Monteur nach dort entsenden. In den		
		Übertrag: RM		588,--

68. 9. 41. 10000. L 0804 (8325)

Document 7 continued.

J. A. TOPF & SÖHNE   4. Blatt des Kostenanschlages vom 3.2.1941.
    ERFURT
        [TOPF]   für   Auschwitz.

Lfd. Nr.	Anzahl	Gegenstand der Veranschlagung			

Übertrag: RM   588,--

Kosten der Montage sind enthalten
die Löhne, Verpflegungsgelder für
den Monteur, sowie das leihweise
Überlassen der für die Monteure not-
wendigen Werkzeuge während der Dauer
der Montage.
Preis   RM   169,--

Gesamtpreis Pos. B 1-7   RM   757,--

Sämtliche Preise verstehen sich ab
unserem Werk Erfurt ausschließlich
Verpackung. Letztere berechnen wir
zu Selbstkosten und nehmen diese
nicht zurück.

Lieferungsbedingungen A.
60.6.40.1000.

68. 9. 40. 10000. L 0204 (3328)

Document 7 continued.

J. A. TOPF & SÖHNE

MASCHINENFABRIK UND FEUERUNGSTECHNISCHES BAUGESCHÄFT

UNSER ARBEITSGEBIET:
Entwurf und Ausführung
vollständiger Kesselhäuser
Verbesserungen u. Umbauten
bei nicht wirtschaftlicher
Dampferzeugung

Abteilung D I
Wärmewirtschaftliche Unter-
suchungen und fachmännische
Beratung
Wärmebilanzen
Eigen-Herstellung und Liefe-
rung sämtlicher wärmetechn.
Anlagen, Apparate und Vor-
richtungen
Topf-Spezial-Feuerungen für
alle Brennstoffe: Steinkohle,
Braunkohle, Schwelkoks, Torf,
Sägespäne, Holz usw.
Vollmechanische Topf-Roste
Halbmech. Topf-Feuerungen
Topf-Wurfbeschicker „Ballist"
Topf-Spezial-Roststäbe
Feuerungsarmaturen
Ölfeuerungen für sämtliche
industrielle Betriebe
Vorwärmer, Lufterhitzer,
Dampfüberhitzer, Flugasche-
Ausblase-Vorrichtungen
Zugverstärkungsanlagen
Einmauerungen von Dampf-
kesseln von industriellen Feue-
rungen bis zu den größten
Abmessungen usw.
Industrie-Schornsteinbau bis zu
den größten Abmessungen
Schmiedeeiserne Schornsteine
Industrie-Ofenbau zur Abfallver-
nichtung, Müllverbrennung,
Kabelverwertung, Vercrackung
Feuerbestattungs-Einrich-
tungen mit moderner elek-
trischer- oder Gas-Beheizung

Abteilung D II
Sämtliche Transport-Anlagen
Mechanische Bekohlung und
Entaschung

Abteilung D III
Lüftungstechnische Anlagen
für industrielle Betriebe, Bade-
anstalten, Gaststätten usw.
Absaugeanlagen für Staub,
Späne usw.
Klimaanlagen
Ventilatorenbau

Abteilung E III
Pneumatische Förderanlagen
für Kohle, Asche, Chemikalien,
Getreide und alle luftförder-
fähigen Schüttgüter

Abteilung C
Eisenkonstruktionen und Be-
hälterbau

Form. 68 a 8. 38. 2000 G.

Kosten-Anschlag

60 JAHRE
GEGR. 1878

ERFURT
POSTFACH 552/₈
FABRIK UND VERWALTUNG
DREYSESTRASSE 7/₉

DRAHTWORT
TOPFWERKE ERFURT

FERNRUF
251 25 251 36 251 27 251 28

UNSERE ABTEILUNG
D/Schu.

ANGEBOT Nr.
41/191

HAUS-APPARAT

DATUM
24.2.1941

An den
Reichsführer SS
und Chef der deutschen Polizei,
Hauptamt Haushalt und Bauten,
SS-Neubauleitung K.L. Auschwitz-Oberschl.

A u s c h w i t z

Betrifft: Entlüftungs-Anlage

Aufgestellt: Schu./we.

Geprüft:

Die Spezialfabrik für feuerungstechnische Anlagen TOPF
hat Zehntausende von TOPF-Feuerungen geliefert.
Hervorragende sechzigjährige Spezialerfahrungen.
Eigene Versuchsstation und feuerungstechnisches Laboratorium.
Untersuchung von Brennstoffen, Asche, Speisewasser.
Eigene Lehrheizer.

Document 8: *Cost estimate by Topf for "ventilation device" (of Crematorium I), dated February 24, 1941. RGVA, 502-1-327, pp. 195-197.*

J. A. TOPF & SOHNE
ERFURT

TOPF

Lfd. Nr.	Anzahl	Gegenstand der Veranschlagung		
I.	1	**Gebläse Nr. 550** zur Förderung von stündlich 8600 cbm Abluft gegen eine Gesamtpressung von 30 mm WS bei einer Umdrehungszahl des Schaufelrades von 700/min. und einem Kraftbedarf an der Welle gemessen von 2,6 PS. Das Gebläse besteht aus einem schmiedeeisernen Gehäuse, einem Schaufelrad, welches fliegend auf Motorwellenstumpf aufgebaut wird, und einem Motorständer. RM	210.--
	1	**Drehstrom-Motor** für 220/380 Volt, 50 Hz. in vollkommen geschlossener Ausführung, mantelgekühlt für eine Leistung von 3 PS bei n = 700/min, mit freiem Wellenende und Doppelnutanker. RM	252.--
	1	**Motorschutzschalter** in gussgekapselter Ausführung mit eingebauter thermischer Überstrom-Auslösung. RM	70.--
	1	**Sterndreieckschalter,** gussgekapselt, ohne Sicherung. RM	15.--
	1	**schmiedeeisernes Konsol,** hergestellt aus kräftigem Profileisen für die erhöhte Aufstellung des Abluftgebläses. RM	90.--
	1	**Abluft-Rohrleitung** 550-160 mm Durchmesser, einschliesslich der Rohrabzweige, der perforierten Luftansaugerohre, 2 Gitter mit Jalousieklappen-Verschluss für den Sezierraum, einschliesslich Mitlieferung der erforderlichen Rohrverbindungen und Rohraufhängungen. RM	1185.--
	1	**Druckstutzen** zur Verbindung der Ausblaseöffnung des Gebläses mit dem vorhandenen gemauerten Schornstein. RM	36.--
		RM	1804.--

68. 1. 40. 8000. Cr.

Document 8 continued.

J. A. TOPF & SÖHNE
E R F U R T

2. Blatt des Kostenanschlages vom 21.7.1941

für   A u s c h w i t z

Lfd. Nr.	Anzahl	Gegenstand der Veranschlagung		
II.		<u>Montage der Anlage,</u> wofür wir einen Monteur nach dort entsenden, jedoch ausschliesslich der Hilfskräfte. In den Kosten der Montage sind enthalten die Löhne, Verpflegungs- und Fahrgelder für den Monteur, die Kosten für die leihweise Überlassung des notwen- digen Werkzeuges während der Dauer der Montage. RM		896.--
		Im Übrigen versteht sich der Preis unseres Kostenanschlages ab Werk, ausschliesslich Verpackung. Letztere berechnen wir zu Selbstkosten und nehmen diese nicht zurück. Lieferzeit: ca. 5 Monate nach Auf- tragseingang und Klar- stellung aller technischen Einzelheiten.		
		Lief.Bed.A. 5o.5.4o.1ooo I o2o4(4o85)		

88. 1. 40. 8000. Cr.

Document 8 continued.

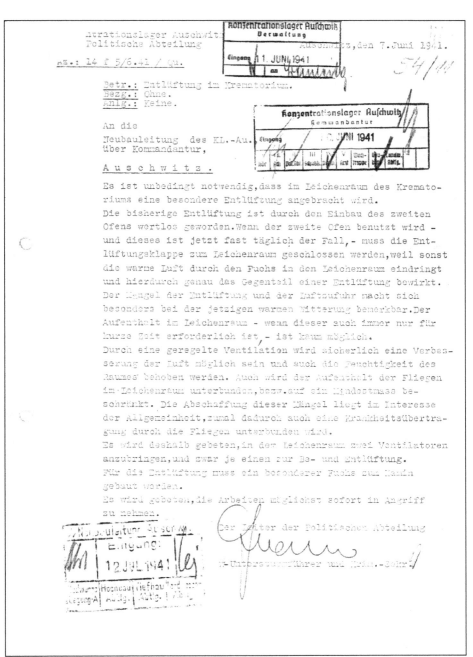

Document 9: *Letter from SS-Untersturmführer Maximilian Grabner to SS-Neubauleitung, dated June 7, 1941. RGVA, 502-1-312, p. 111.*

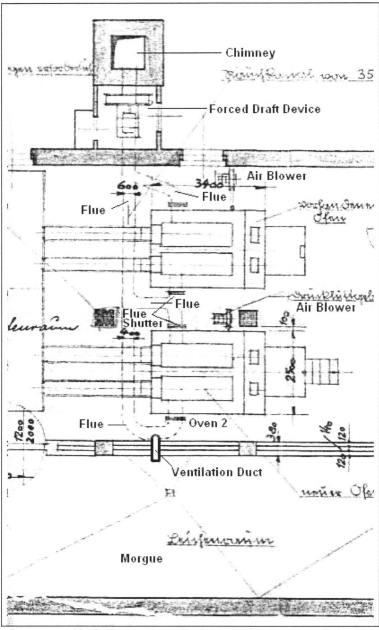

Document 10: *Author's schematic drawing of first, makeshift ventilation installation for morgue of Crematorium I at Auschwitz, horizontal section, drawn onto Topf drawing D 57999, dated November 30, 1940, with English labels added.*

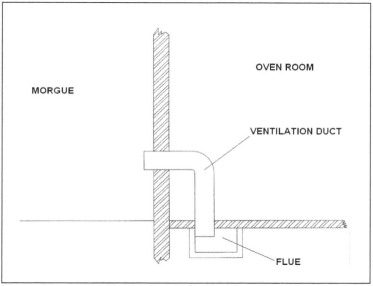

Document 11: *Schematic diagram of first, makeshift ventilation installation for morgue of Crematorium I at Auschwitz. Vertical section.* © Carlo Mattogno

SS-Neubauleitung K. L. Auschwitz
Häftlings-Schlosserei
Eingang am 25 SEP 1941

Aufbrag Nr. 1714

Drincl.-Grad

Arbeitskarte

Kolonne _Zaleski_ *BW.M*

Gegenstand 4 st. Luftdichte - Klappen anfertigen

Antragsteller Krematorium

Angefangen 25. IX. 1941 Beendet 25. IX. 1941

	Nr.	Name	Arbeitszeit Std.	Min.		Nr.	Name	Arbeitszeit Std.	Min.
Schlosser	8363	Zalewski	3	/	Schweisser	1961	Bialos	1	/
	7686	Morgiel	5	/					
	16197	Dudzinski	2	/					
					Dreher				
					Schmiede				
		Ablegen!					22/10 41		
					Klempner				
					Installateure				
Giesser								18,40 U.	

Insgesamt 11 Arbeitsstunden – davon 1 Schweisserstunden.

Document 12: *Inmate locksmith shop, labor card, September 25, 1941, order no. 1714. RGVA, 502-2-1, pp. 74, 74a.*

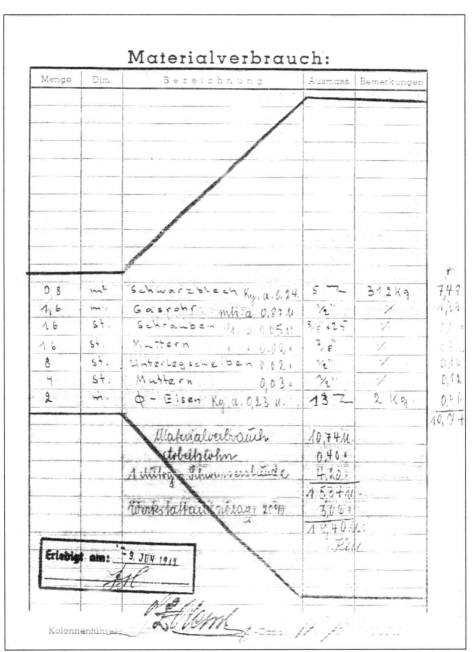

Materialverbrauch:

Menge	Dim.	Bezeichnung	Ausmass	Bemerkungen	
0,8	m²	Schwarzblech Kg. a. 6,24	5	31,2 Kg	7,49
1,6	m	Gasrohr m/h a 0,87 u	½"		1,37
16	St.	Schrauben a 0,05 u	⅜ x 25		
16	St.	Muttern 0,02	⅜"		
8	St.	Unterlegscheiben 0,02	½"		0,16
4	St.	Muttern 0,03	½"		0,12
2	m	⌀ - Eisen Kg. a 0,23 u	13	2 Kg.	0,46
					10,74

	Materialverbrauch	10,74 u	
	Arbeitslohn	0,46 u	
	Anteilige Unkostenstände	4,20 u	
		15,40 u	
	Werkstattunkosten 20%	3,06 u	
		18,40 u	

Erledigt am: 9. JUN 1943

Kolonnenführer: .... J.-Capo: ....

Document 12 continued.

SS-Neubauleitung K. L. Auschwitz
Häftlings-Schlosserei

Eingang am ___ 7. OKT. 1941

Auftrag Nr. *1760*

Dringl.-Grad ___

Arbeitskarte

Kolonne _Szabelewski_

Gegenstand Anfertigen von 2 Stück Entlüftungs-
häten aus Eisenblech 27 × 27 cm I.L.
sonst nach Angabe

Antragsteller _Krematorium_

Angefangen: 7. X. 1941   Beendet 13. X. 1941.

	Nr.	Name	Arbeitszeit Std. Min.		Nr.	Name	Arbeitszeit Std. Min.
Schlosser				Schweisser	1461	Bielers	2 /
				Dreher			
				Schmiede			
				Klempner	9612	Maliszewski	24 /
					1409	Dyntar	24 /
				Installateure			
Giesser							26,75 M.

Ablegen!

Insgesamt __50__ Arbeitsstunden – davon __2__ Schweisserstunden.

Document 13: Inmate locksmith shop, labor card, October 7, 1941, order no. 1760.
RGVA, 502-2-1, pp. 75,75a.

Der Luftschutzleiter

Az.LS 217 - Jo/B

Betrifft: Ausbau des alten Krematoriums für Luftschutzwecke

Anlagen: 1 Plan.

Konzentrationslager Auschwitz
Bauleitung

Auschwitz O/S,den 26.August 1944.-

An den

SS-Standortältesten als örtl.
Luftschutzleiter

A u s c h w i t z O/S

In der Anlage überreiche ich einen Plan über den Ausbau des
alten Krematoriums für Luftschutzwecke mit der Bitte um Geneh-
migung dieses Ausbaues.

1.Arbeitsvorgänge:

Abbruch der alten Kammeröfen und reinigen der dabei anfallen-
den Ziegel zwecks Wiederverwendung,
Auffüllen der Heizschächte und Heizkanäle mit dem beim Ab-
bruch der Kammeröfen anfallendem Schutt und Altmaterial,
Durchbruch der Fenster-und Türöffnungen,
Einsetzen der Gasschutztüren,Fensterblenden und Fenster,
Herstellung der für die Beheizungsöfen,sowie für die Ent-und
Belüftung erforderlichen Mauerdurchbrüche und Schläuche,
Wasserinstallations-und Kanalisationsarbeiter,
Verlegen der vorhandenen Lichtleitungen entsprechend der
Raumeinteilung,
Ausbesserung der Fußböden und Teilverlegung eines Holzfuß-
bodens,
Ausbesserung des Daches und Anstrich desselben mit Gudron.

2.Materialbedarf:

500 kg Zement,
400 kg Ziegel,
 20 kg Rundeisen,
 50 m Eisenbahnschienen,
 24 St Kanthölzer 10/15 cm,4,80 m lang,
 10 St Kanthölzer 10/15 cm,3,90 m lang,
102 m² Bretter 25 mm stark,
 13 St Fenster einflügelig 60 X 80 cm,
  2 St Türen einflügelig 70 X 200 cm.
 16 St Fensterblenden gas-und splittersicher,
  7 St Türen gas-und splittersicher.

Der Luftschutzleiter:

SS-Obersturmführer

Document 14: *Letter from SS-Obersturmführer Josten "to the SS garrison eldest as local head of air-raid protection," dated August 26, 1944. RGVA, 502-1-401, p. 34.*

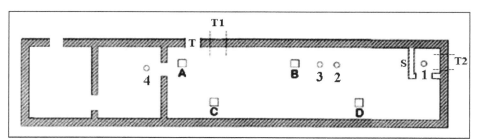

Document 15: *Drawing of the morgue of Crematorium I with rooms to the left (original state). A,B,C,D: position of current openings in the roof. 1, 2, 3, 4: position of original circular openings, today closed. T: original door to the furnace room; T1: position of current opening to the furnace room; T2: Current access door from the outside; S: Current vestibule, included when converted into an air raid shelter.* © Carlo Mattogno

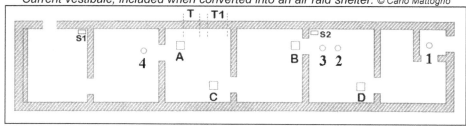

Document 16: *Drawing of the morgue with rooms to the left after conversion to air raid shelter. A,B,C,D: position of current openings in the roof. 1, 2, 3, 4: position of original circular openings, today closed. T: original door to the furnace room. T1: current opening (both were closed during the use of this facility as an air raid shelter). S1, S2: position of air raid shelter's ventilation shafts.* © Carlo Mattogno

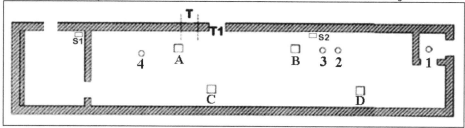

Document 17: *Drawing of the morgue with room to the left, current situation. A,B,C,D: position of current openings in the roof. 1, 2, 3, 4: position of original circular openings, today closed. T: position of original door to the furnace room. T1: current opening. S1, S2: position of ventilation shafts.* © Carlo Mattogno

Document 18: *The roof of Crematorium I, photo taken by Stanisław Luczko (probably in May 1945).[324] 1,2,3,4: dark spots on the roof felt. The added line links the left-hand sides of spots no. 1 and 4.* © Carlo Mattogno

Document 19: *Photo of opening no. 1 in the roof of the vestibule, part of the former morgue.* © Carlo Mattogno

Document 20: *Photo of opening no. 2 in the roof of the morgue.* © Carlo Mattogno

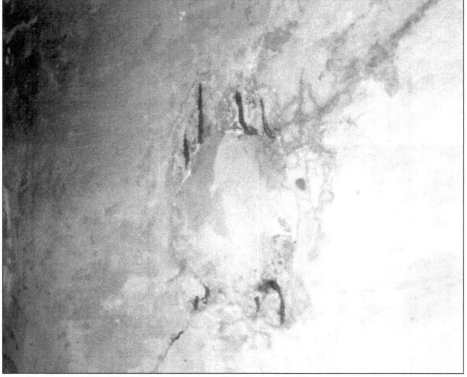

Document 21: *Photo of opening no. 3 in the roof of the morgue.* © Carlo Mattogno

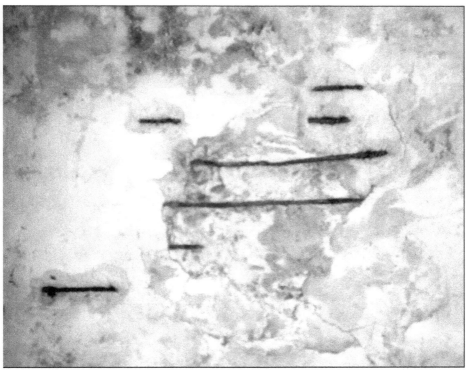

Document 22: *Photo of opening no. 4 in the roof of the washing room.* © Carlo Mattogno

Document 23: *Photo of the roof of the morgue. All four shafts constructed by the Poles after the war.* © Carlo Mattogno

Document 24: *Photo of the roof of the morgue. One of the four shafts constructed by the Poles after the war.* © Carlo Mattogno

Document 25: *Photo of the ceiling of the morgue. One of the four shafts constructed by the Poles after the war.* © Carlo Mattogno

Document 26: *Auschwitz, old crematorium seen from north-west.*
© Fredrick Töben 1997

Document 27: *Auschwitz, old crematorium, close-up.* © Carlo Mattogno 1991

Document 28: *Auschwitz, old crematorium, interior of the former morgue plus washing room.* © *Carlo Mattogno 1992*

Document 29: *Auschwitz, old crematorium, second cremation furnace (reconstructed by the Poles) and current access opening to the former morgue (equally created by the Poles).* © *Fredrick Töben 1997*

Document 30: *Auschwitz, old crematorium, gas-tight door of the air-raid shelter (rear entry); at the right: wooden door of the vestibule.* © Fredrick Töben 1997

Document 31: *Auschwitz, old crematorium, probably the gas-tight door temporarily separating the air-raid shelter from the former furnace room, in 1991 stored in the furnace room.* © Carlo Mattogno 1991

Document 33: Gas-tight wooden door found in 1945 in the vicinity of Crematorium V at Birkenau and preserved at the old crematorium at Auschwitz. (See Document 32). © Carlo Mattogno 1992

Document 32: Gas-tight wooden door found in the vicinity of Crematorium V at Birkenau. Polish photo of April-May 1945. APMO, microfilm no. 12683.

Document 34: *Auschwitz, old crematorium, door with glass window separating to-day's "gas chamber," but originally the former washing room, from the former laying-out/surgery room.* © Fredrick Töben 1997

Document 35: *Auschwitz, old crematorium, toilet drains of former air-raid shelter, now located in what is claimed to have been a "gas chamber."* © Fredrick Töben 1997

Abbreviations

AGK   Archiwum Głównej Komisji Badania Zbrodni Przeciwko
       Narodowi Polskiemu Instytutu Pamieci Narodowej (Archive of
       the Central Commission of Inquiry into the Crimes against the
       Polish People – National Memorial), Warsaw
APMM   Archiwum Państwowego Muzeum na Majdanku (Archive of State
       Museum at Majdanek)
APMO   Archiwum Państwowego Muzeum Oświęcim-Brzezinka (Archive
       of the State Museum at Auschwitz-Birkenau)
BAK   Bundesarchiv Koblenz
GARF   Gosudarstvenni Archiv Rossiskoi Federatsii (State Archive of the
       Russian Federation), Moscow
PRO   Public Record Office, Kew, Richmond, Surrey, Great Britain
RGVA   Rossiiskii Gosudarstvennii Vojennii Archiv (Russian State War
       Archive), Moscow
ZStL   Zentrale Stelle der Landesjustizverwaltungen, Ludwigsburg

Bibliography

– Aynat, Enrique, "Neither Trace nor Proof: The Seven Auschwitz 'Gassing' Sites
  According to Jean-Claude Pressac," *Journal of Historical Review* 11(2) (1991),
  pp. 177-206
– Baum, Bruno, *Widerstand in Auschwitz. Bericht der internationalen antifaschis-
  tischen Lagerleitung*, VVN-Verlag, Berlin-Potsdam 1949
– Bezwinska, Jadwiga, Danuta Czech (eds.), *Auschwitz in den Augen der SS*,
  Staatliches Museum Auschwitz-Birkenau, 1997
– Broad, Pery, "KZ-Auschwitz. Erinnerungen eines SS-Mannes der Politischen
  Abteilung in dem Konzentrationslager Auschwitz", in: *Hefte von Auschwitz.*
  Wydawnictwo Państwowego Muzeum w Oświęciumiu, 9, 1966, S. 7-48
– Broszat, Martin (ed.), *Kommandant in Auschwitz. Autobiographische Aufzeich-
  nungen des Rudolf Höss*, Deutscher Taschenbuch Verlag, Munich 1981
– Central Commission for the Investigation of Hitlerian Crimes in Poland (ed.),
  Wspomnienia Rudolfa Hössa komendanta obozu oświęmciskiego, Wydawnictwo
  Prawnicze, Warsaw 1956
– Czech, Danuta, *Kalendarium der Ereignisse im Konzentrationslager Auschwitz-
  Birkenau 1939–1945,* Rowohlt Verlag, Reinbek, Germany 1989
– Deutsche Gesellschaft für Schädlingsbekämpfung m.b.H., *Fumigation Cham-
  bers for Pest Control*, Erasmus Druck Mainz, 1967
– Długoborski, Wacław, Franciszek Piper (eds.), *Auschwitz 1940-1945. Central
  Issues in the History of the Camp*, Auschwitz-Birkenau State Museum 2000

– Długoborski, Wacław, Franciszek Piper (eds.), *Auschwitz 1940-1945. Węzłowe zagadnienia z dziejów obozu.* Wydawnictwo Państwowego Muzeum Oświęcim-Brzezinka, 1995, vol. III, *Zagłada*
– Dwork, Deborah, Robert J. van Pelt, *Auschwitz 1270 to the Present*, W.W. Norton & Company, New York-London 1996
– Friedman, Filip, *This Was Oswiecim. The History of a Murder Camp*, The United Jewish Relief Appeal, London 1946
– Graf, Jürgen, Thomas Kues, Carlo Mattogno, *Sobibór: Holocaust Propaganda and Reality*, The Barnes Review, Washington, DC, 2010
– Gutman, Israel, Michael Berenbaum (eds.), *Anatomy of the Auschwitz Death Camp*, Indiana University Press, Bloomington/Indianapolis 1994
– Keren, Daniel, Jamie McCarthy, Harry W. Mazal, "The Ruins of the Gas Chambers: A Forensic Investigation of Crematoriums at Auschwitz I and Auschwitz-Birkenau," in: *Holocaust and Genocide Studies*, Vol. 9, No. 1, Spring 2004
– Kraus, Ota, Erich Kulka, *Die Todesfabrik*, Kongress-Verlag, Berlin 1958
– Langbein, Hermann, *Der Auschwitz-Prozess. Eine Dokumentation*, Europa Verlag, Vienna 1965
– Lenz, Otto, Ludwig Gaßner, *Schädlingsbekämpfung mit hochgiftigen Stoffen.* issue no. 1: "Blausäure," Verlagsbuchhandlung von Richard Schoetz, Berlin 1934
– Lettich, André, *Trente-quatre mois dans les Camps de Concentration. Témoignage sur les crimes "scientifiques" commis par les médecins allemands*, Imprimerie Union Coopérative, Tours 1946
– Leuchter, Fred A., *An Engineering Report on the Alleged Execution Gas Chambers at Auschwitz, Birkenau and Majdanek, Poland*, Samisdat Publishers, Toronto 1988
– Leuchter, Fred A., Robert Faurisson, Germar Rudolf, *The Leuchter Reports. Critical Edition*, 4th ed., Castle Hill Publishers, Uckfield 2015
– Markiewicz, Jan, Wojciech Gubała, Jerzy Łabędź, "A study of the cyanide compounds content in the walls of the gas chambers in the former Auschwitz and Birkenau concentration camps", *Z Zagadnień Nauk Sądowych*, Jg. XXX, 1994, pp. 17-27
– Mattogno, Carlo, "Auschwitz: 'Gas Testers' and Gas Residue Test Kits," in: *The Revisionist*, 2(2) (May 2004), pp. 150-155
– Mattogno, Carlo, "Flames and Smoke from the Chimneys of Crematoria," *he Revisionist*, 2(1) (2004), pp. 73-78
– Mattogno, Carlo, *Auschwitz: Die erste Vergasung. Gerücht und Wirklichkeit*, 2nd ed., Castle Hill Publishers, Uckfield 2014
– Mattogno, Carlo, *Auschwitz: la prima gasazione*. Edizioni di Ar, Padua, 1992
– Mattogno, Carlo, *Auschwitz: The First Gassing. Rumor and Reality*, 3rd ed., Castle Hill Publishers, Uckfield 2016
– Mattogno, Carlo, *Bełżec in Propaganda, Testimonies, Archeological Research, and History*, Theses & Dissertations Press, Chicago 2004
– Mattogno, Carlo, *Debunking the Bunkers of Auschwitz: Black Propaganda versus History*, 2nd ed., Castle Hill Publishers, Uckfield 2016

– Mattogno, Carlo, *Olocausto: Dilettanti allo sbaraglio.* Edizioni di Ar, Padua 1996
– Mattogno, Carlo, *Special Treatment in Auschwitz: Origin and Meaning of a Term*, 2nd ed., Castle Hill Publishers, Uckfield 2016
– Mattogno, Carlo, *The Central Construction Office of the Waffen-SS and Police Auschwitz. Organization, Responsibilities, Activities*, Theses & Dissertations Press, Chicago 2005
– Mattogno, Carlo, Franco Deana, *The Cremation Furnaces of Auschwitz: A Technical and Historical Study*, Castle Hill Publishers, Uckfield 2015
– Mattogno, Carlo, Jürgen Graf, *Treblinka: Extermination Camp or Transit Camp?* Theses & Dissertations Press, Chicago 2004
– Müller, Filip, *Sonderbehandlung. Drei Jahre in den Krematorien und Gaskammern von Auschwitz*, Verlag Steinhausen, Munich 1979
– "Obóz koncentracyjny Oświęcim w świetle akt Delegatury Rządu R.P. na Kraj", *Zeszyty oświęcimskie*, Special Edition I. Wydawnictwo Państwowego Muzeum w Oświęcimiu, Auschwitz 1968
– Pressac, Jean-Claude, *Auschwitz: Technique and operation of the gas chambers*, The Beate Klarsfeld Foundation, New York 1989
– Pressac, Jean-Claude, *Die Krematorien von Auschwitz. Die Technik des Massenmordes*, Piper, Munich, Zürich 1994
– Pressac, Jean-Claude, *Les crématoires d'Auschwitz. La machinerie du meurtre de masse*, CNRS Editions, Paris 1993
– Rudolf, Germar, "From the Records of the Frankfurt Auschwitz Trial, Part 7," *The Revisionist* 3(1) (2005), pp. 92-97
– Rudolf, Germar, *The Rudolf Report*, 2nd ed., The Barnes Review, Washington, D.C., 2011
– Saletti, Carlo (ed.), *Testimoni della catastrofe. Deposizioni di prigionieri del Sonderkommando ebraico di Auschwitz-Birkenau (1945)*, Ombre corte, Verona 2004
– Schumacher, Fritz, *Die Feuerbestattung*, J.M. Gebhardt's Verlag, Leipzig 1938
– Sehn, Jan, *Oświęcim-Brzezinka (Auschwitz-Birkenau) Concentration camp*, Wydawnictwo Prawnicze, Warsaw 1961
– Sehn, Jan, "Obóz koncentracyjny i zagłady Oświęcim", in: *Biuletyn Głównej Komisji Badania Zbrodni Niemieckich w Polsce*, Bd. I, Posen 1946, pp. 63-130
– State Museum Auschwitz (ed.), *Auschwitz (Oświęcim): Camp hitlérien d'extermination*, Editions Interpress, Warsaw 1978
– State Museum Auschwitz (ed.), *Auschwitz vu par les SS*, Edition du Musée d'Etat à Oświęcim, 1974
– State Museum Auschwitz, "Inmitten des grauenvollen Verbrechens. Handschriften von Mitgliedern des *Sonderkommando*s." *Hefte von Auschwitz*, Sonderheft I. Verlag des Staatlichen Auschwitz-Birkenau Museums, Auschwitz 1972
– State Museum Auschwitz-Birkenau (ed.), *Sterbebücher von Auschwitz*, K.G. Saur, Munich/New Providence/London/Paris 1995
– van Pelt, Robert J., *The Case for Auschwitz: Evidence from the Irving Trial.* Indiana University Press, Bloomington/Indianapolis 2002

Index of Names

Individuals only, except for the inmates listed in Tables 1, p. 31. Entries from footnotes in italics.

HOLOCAUST HANDBOOKS

T his ambitious, growing series addresses various aspects of the "Holocaust" of the WWII era. Most of them are based on decades of research from archives all over the world. They are heavily referenced. In contrast to most other works on this issue, the tomes of this series approach its topic with profound academic scrutiny and a critical attitude. Any Holocaust researcher ignoring this series will remain oblivious to some of the most important research in the field. These books are designed to both convince the common reader as well as academics. The following books have appeared so far, or are about to be released. Compare hardcopy and eBook prices at www.findbookprices.com.

SECTION ONE:
General Overviews of the Holocaust

The First Holocaust. The Surprising Origin of the Six-Million Figure. By Don Heddesheimer.

This compact but substantive study documents

propaganda spread prior to, during and after the FIRST World War that claimed East European Jewry was on the brink of annihilation. The magic number of suffering and dying Jews was 6 million back then as well. The book details how these Jewish fundraising operations in America raised vast sums in the name of feeding suffering Polish and Russian Jews but actually funneled much of the money to Zionist and Communist groups. 5th ed., 200 pages, b&w illustrations, bibliography, index. (#6)

Pictured above are all of the scientific studies that comprise the series *Holocaust Handbooks* published thus far or are about to be released. More volumes and new editions are constantly in the works. Check www.HolocaustHandbooks.com for updates.

Lectures on the Holocaust. Controversial Issues Cross Examined. By Germar Rudolf.

This book first explains why "the Holocaust" is an important topic, and that it is essential to keep an open mind about it. It then tells how

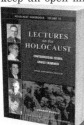

many mainstream scholars expressed doubts and subsequently fell from grace. Next, the physical traces and documents about the various claimed crime scenes and murder weapons are discussed. After that, the reliability of witness testimony is examined. Finally, the author argues for a free exchange of ideas on this topic. This book gives the most-comprehensive and up-to-date overview of the critical research into the Holocaust. With its dialogue style, it is easy to read, and it can even be used as an encyclopedic compendium. 3rd ed., 596 pages, b&w illustrations, bibliography, index.(#15)

Breaking the Spell. The Holocaust, Myth & Reality. By Nicholas Kollerstrom. In 1941,

British Intelligence analysts cracked the German "Enigma" code. Hence, in 1942 and 1943, encrypted radio communications between German concentration camps and the Berlin headquarters were decrypted. The intercepted data refutes the orthodox "Holocaust" narrative. It reveals that the Germans were desperate to reduce the death rate in their labor camps, which was caused by catastrophic typhus epidemics. Dr. Kollerstrom, a science historian, has taken these intercepts and a wide array of mostly unchallenged corroborating evidence to show that "witness statements" supporting the human gas chamber narrative clearly clash with the available scientific data. Kollerstrom concludes that

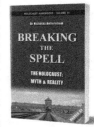

the history of the Nazi "Holocaust" has been written by the victors with ulterior motives. It is distorted, exaggerated and largely wrong. With a foreword by Prof. Dr. James Fetzer. 5th ed., 282 pages, b&w ill., bibl., index. (#31)

Debating the Holocaust. A New Look at Both Sides. By Thomas Dalton. Mainstream histo-

rians insist that there cannot be, may not be, any debate about the Holocaust. But ignoring it does not make this controversy go away. Traditional scholars admit that there was neither a budget, a plan, nor an order for the Holocaust; that the key camps have all but vanished, and so have any human remains; that material and unequivocal documentary evidence is absent; and that there are serious problems with survivor testimonies. Dalton juxtaposes the traditional Holocaust narrative with revisionist challenges and then analyzes the mainstream's responses to them. He reveals the weaknesses of both sides, while declaring revisionism the winner of the current state

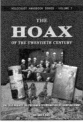

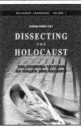

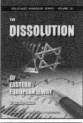

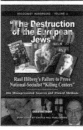

of the debate. 4th ed., 342 pages, b&w illustrations, bibliography, index. (#32)

The Hoax of the Twentieth Century. The Case against the Presumed Extermination of European Jewry.

By Arthur R. Butz. The first writer to analyze the entire Holocaust complex in a precise scientific manner. This book exhibits the overwhelming force of arguments accumulated by the mid-1970s. Butz's two main arguments are: 1. All major entities hostile to Germany must have known what was happening to the Jews under German authority. They acted during the war as if no mass slaughter was occurring. 2. All the evidence adduced to prove any mass slaughter has a dual interpretation, while only the innocuous one can be proven to be correct. This book continues to be a major historical reference work, frequently cited by prominent personalities. This edition has numerous supplements with new information gathered over the last 35 years. 4th ed., 524 pages, b&w illustrations, bibliography, index. (#7)

Dissecting the Holocaust. The Growing Critique of 'Truth' and 'Memory.'

Edited by Germar Rudolf. *Dissecting the Holocaust* applies state-of-the-art scientific techniques and classic methods of detection to investigate the alleged murder of millions of Jews by Germans during World War II. In 22 contributions—each of some 30 pages—the 17 authors dissect generally accepted paradigms of the "Holocaust." It reads as excitingly as a crime novel: so many lies, forgeries and deceptions by politicians, historians and scientists are proven. This is the intellectual adventure of the 21st Century. Be part of it! 3rd ed., 635 pages, b&w illustrations, bibliography, index. (#1)

The Dissolution of Eastern European Jewry.

By Walter N. Sanning. Six Million Jews died in the Holocaust. Sanning did not take that number at face value, but thoroughly explored European population developments and shifts mainly caused by emigration as well as deportations and evacuations conducted by both Nazis and the Soviets, among other things. The book is based mainly on Jewish, Zionist and mainstream sources. It concludes that a sizeable share of the Jews found missing during local censuses after the Second World War, which were so far counted as "Holocaust victims," had either emigrated (mainly to Israel or the U.S.) or had been deported by Stalin to Siberian labor camps. 2nd ed., foreword by A.R. Butz, epilogue by Germar Rudolf containing important

updates; 224 pages, b&w illustrations, bibliography (#29).

Air-Photo Evidence: World-War-Two Photos of Alleged Mass-Murder Sites Analyzed.

By Germar Rudolf (editor). During World War Two both German and Allied reconnaissance aircraft took countless air photos of places of tactical and strategic interest in Europe. These photos are prime evidence for the investigation of the Holocaust. Air photos of locations like Auschwitz, Majdanek, Treblinka, Babi Yar etc. permit an insight into what did or did not happen there. The author has unearthed many pertinent photos and has thoroughly analyzed them. This book is full of air-photo reproductions and schematic drawings explaining them. According to the author, these images refute many of the atrocity claims made by witnesses in connection with events in the German sphere of influence. 6th edition; with a contribution by Carlo Mattogno. 167 pages, 8.5"×11", b&w illustrations, bibliography, index (#27).

The Leuchter Reports: Critical Edition.

By Fred Leuchter, Robert Faurisson and Germar Rudolf. Between 1988 and 1991, U.S. expert on execution technologies Fred Leuchter wrote four reports on whether the Third Reich operated homicidal gas chambers. The first on Auschwitz and Majdanek became world-famous. Based on various arguments, Leuchter concluded that the locations investigated could never have been "utilized or seriously considered to function as execution gas chambers." The second report deals with gas-chamber claims for the camps Dachau, Mauthausen and Hartheim, while the third reviews design criteria and operation procedures of execution gas chambers in the U.S. The fourth report reviews Pressac's 1989 tome about Auschwitz. 4th ed., 252 pages, b&w illustrations. (#16)

Bungled: "The Destruction of the European Jews". Raul Hilberg's Failure to Prove National-Socialist "Killing Centers."

By Carlo Mattogno. Raul Hilberg's magnum opus *The Destruction of the European Jews* is an orthodox standard work on the Holocaust. But how does Hilberg support his thesis that Jews were murdered *en masse*? He rips documents out of their context, distorts their content, misinterprets their meaning, and ignores entire archives. He only refers to "useful" witnesses, quotes fragments out of context, and conceals the fact that his witnesses are lying through their teeth. Lies and deceits permeate Hilberg's book, 302 pages, bibliography, index. (#3)

Jewish Emigration from the Third Reich. By Ingrid Weckert. Current historical writings about the Third Reich claim state it was difficult for Jews to flee from Nazi persecution. The truth is that Jewish emigration was welcomed by the German authorities. Emigration was not some kind of wild flight, but rather a lawfully determined and regulated matter. Weckert's booklet elucidates the emigration process in law and policy. She shows that German and Jewish authorities worked closely together. Jews interested in emigrating received detailed advice and offers of help from both sides. 2nd ed., 130 pages, index. (#12)

Inside the Gas Chambers: The Extermination of Mainstream Holocaust Historiography. By Carlo Mattogno. Neither increased media propaganda or political pressure nor judicial persecution can stifle revisionism. Hence, in early 2011, the Holocaust Orthodoxy published a 400-page book (in German) claiming to refute "revisionist propaganda," trying again to prove "once and for all" that there were homicidal gas chambers at the camps of Dachau, Natzweiler, Sachsenhausen, Mauthausen, Ravensbrück, Neuengamme, Stutthof... you name them. Mattogno shows with his detailed analysis of this work of propaganda that mainstream Holocaust hagiography is beating around the bush rather than addressing revisionist research results. He exposes their myths, distortions and lies. 2nd ed., 280 pages, b&w illustrations, bibliography, index. (#25)

SECTION TWO:
Specific non-Auschwitz Studies

Treblinka: Extermination Camp or Transit Camp? By Carlo Mattogno and Jürgen Graf. It is alleged that at Treblinka in East Poland between 700,000 and 3,000,000 persons were murdered in 1942 and 1943. The weapons used were said to have been stationary and/ or mobile gas chambers, fast-acting or slow-acting poison gas, unslaked lime, superheated steam, electricity, Diesel-exhaust fumes etc. Holocaust historians alleged that bodies were piled as high as multi-storied buildings and burned without a trace, using little or no fuel at all. Graf and Mattogno have now analyzed the origins, logic and technical feasibility of the official version of Treblinka. On the basis of numerous documents they reveal Treblinka's true identity as a mere transit

camp. 3rd ed., 384 pages, b&w illustrations, bibliography, index. (#8)

Belzec: Propaganda, Testimonies, Archeological Research and History. By Carlo Mattogno. Witnesses report that between 600,000 and 3 million Jews were murdered in the Belzec Camp, located in Poland. Various murder weapons are claimed to have been used: Diesel-exhaust gas; unslaked lime in trains; high voltage; vacuum chambers; etc. The corpses were incinerated on huge pyres without leaving a trace. For those who know the stories about Treblinka this sounds familiar. Thus the author has restricted this study to the aspects which are new compared to Treblinka. In contrast to Treblinka, forensic drillings and excavations were performed at Belzec, the results of which are critically reviewed. 142 pages, b&w illustrations, bibliography, index. (#9)

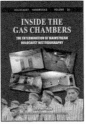

Sobibor: Holocaust Propaganda and Reality. By Jürgen Graf, Thomas Kues and Carlo Mattogno. Between 25,000 and 2 million Jews are said to have been killed in gas chambers in the Sobibór camp in Poland. The corpses were allegedly buried in mass graves and later incinerated on pyres. This book investigates these claims and shows that they are based on the selective use of contradictory eyewitness testimony. Archeological surveys of the camp are analyzed that started in 2000-2001 and carried on until 2018. The book also documents the general National-Socialist policy toward Jews, which never included a genocidal "final solution." 2nd ed., 456 pages, b&w illustrations, bibliography, index. (#19)

The "Operation Reinhardt" Camps Treblinka, Sobibór, Bełżec. By Carlo Mattogno. As an update and upgrade to the Volumes 8, 9 and 19 of this series, this study has its first focus on witness testimonies recorded during the World War II and the immediate post-war era, many of them discussed here for the first time, thus demonstrating how the myth of the "extermination camps" was created. The second part of this book brings us up to speed with the various archeological efforts made by mainstream scholars in their attempt to prove that the myth based on testimonies is true. The third part compares the findings of the second part with what we ought to expect, and reveals the chasm that exists between archeologically proven facts and mythological requirements. 402 pages, illustrations, bibliography, index. (#28)

Chelmno: A Camp in History & Propaganda. By Carlo Mattogno. At Chelmno, huge masses of Jewish prisoners are said to have been gassed in "gas vans" or shot (claims vary from 10,000 to 1.3 million victims). This study covers the subject from every angle, undermining the orthodox claims about the camp with an overwhelmingly effective body of evidence. Eyewitness statements, gas wagons as extermination weapons, forensics reports and excavations, German documents—all come under Mattogno's scrutiny. Here are the uncensored facts about Chelmno, not the propaganda. 2nd ed., 188 pages, indexed, illustrated, bibliography. (#23)

The Gas Vans: A Critical Investigation. By Santiago Alvarez and Pierre Marais. It is alleged that the Nazis used mobile gas chambers to exterminate 700,000 people. Up until 2011, no thorough monograph had appeared on the topic. Santiago Alvarez has remedied the situation. Are witness statements believable? Are documents genuine? Where are the murder weapons? Could they have operated as claimed? Where are the corpses? In order to get to the truth of the matter, Alvarez has scrutinized all known wartime documents and photos about this topic; he has analyzed a huge amount of witness statements as published in the literature and as presented in more than 30 trials held over the decades in Germany, Poland and Israel; and he has examined the claims made in the pertinent mainstream literature. The result of his research is mind-boggling. Note: This book and Mattogno's book on Chelmno were edited in parallel to make sure they are consistent and not repetitive. 398 pages, b&w illustrations, bibliography, index. (#26)

The Einsatzgruppen in the Occupied Eastern Territories: Genesis, Missions and Actions. By C. Mattogno. Before invading the Soviet Union, the German authorities set up special units meant to secure the area behind the German front. Orthodox historians claim that these units called *Einsatzgruppen* primarily engaged in rounding up and mass-murdering Jews. This study sheds a critical light onto this topic by reviewing all the pertinent sources as well as material traces. It reveals on the one hand that original war-time documents do not fully support the orthodox genocidal narrative, and on the other that most post-"liberation" sources such as testimonies and forensic reports are steeped in Soviet atrocity propaganda and are thus utterly unreliable. In ad-

dition, material traces of the claimed massacres are rare due to an attitude of collusion by governments and Jewish lobby groups. 830 pp., b&w illustrations, bibliography, index. (#39)

Concentration Camp Majdanek. A Historical and Technical Study. By Carlo Mattogno and Jürgen Graf. At war's end, the Soviets claimed that up to two million Jews were murdered at the Majdanek Camp in seven gas chambers. Over the decades, however, the Majdanek Museum reduced the death toll three times to currently 78,000, and admitted that there were "only" two gas chambers. By exhaustively researching primary sources, the authors expertly dissect and repudiate the myth of homicidal gas chambers at that camp. They also critically investigated the legend of mass executions of Jews in tank trenches and prove it groundless. Again they have produced a standard work of methodical investigation which authentic historiography cannot ignore. 3rd ed., 358 pages, b&w illustrations, bibliography, index. (#5)

Concentration Camp Stutthof and Its Function in National Socialist Jewish Policy. By Carlo Mattogno and Jürgen Graf. Orthodox historians claim that the Stutthof Camp served as a "makeshift" extermination camp in 1944. Based mainly on archival resources, this study thoroughly debunks this view and shows that Stutthof was in fact a center for the organization of German forced labor toward the end of World War II. 4th ed., 170 pages, b&w illustrations, bibliography, index. (#4)

SECTION THREE:
Auschwitz Studies

The Making of the Auschwitz Myth: Auschwitz in British Intercepts, Polish Underground Reports and Postwar Testimonies (1941-1947). By Carlo Mattogno. Using messages sent by the Polish underground to London, SS radio messages sent to and from Auschwitz that were intercepted and decrypted by the British, and a plethora of witness statements made during the war and in the immediate postwar period, the author shows how exactly the myth of mass murder in Auschwitz gas chambers was created, and how it was turned subsequently into "history" by intellectually corrupt scholars who cherry-picked claims that fit into their agenda and ignored or actively covered up literally thousands of lies of "witnesses" to make their narrative look credible. 2nd edition, 514 pp., b&w illustrations, bibliography, index. (#41)

The Real Case of Auschwitz: Robert van Pelt's Evidence from the Irving Trial Critically Reviewed.

By Carlo Mattogno. Prof. Robert van Pelt is considered one of the best mainstream experts on Auschwitz. He became famous when appearing as an expert during the London libel trial of David Irving against Deborah Lipstadt. From it resulted a book titled *The Case for Auschwitz*, in which van Pelt laid out his case for the existence of homicidal gas chambers at that camp. This book is a scholarly response to Prof. van Pelt—and Jean-Claude Pressac, upon whose books van Pelt's study is largely based. Mattogno lists all the evidence van Pelt adduces, and shows one by one that van Pelt misrepresented and misinterpreted every single one of them. This is a book of prime political and scholarly importance to those looking for the truth about Auschwitz. 3rd ed., 692 pages, b&w illustrations, glossary, bibliography, index. (#22)

Auschwitz: Plain Facts: A Response to Jean-Claude Pressac.

Edited by Germar Rudolf, with contributions by Serge Thion, Robert Faurisson and Carlo Mattogno. French pharmacist Jean-Claude Pressac tried to refute revisionist findings with the "technical" method. For this he was praised by the mainstream, and they proclaimed victory over the "revisionists." In his book, Pressac's works and claims are shown to be unscientific in nature, as he never substantiates what he claims, and historically false, because he systematically misrepresents, misinterprets and misunderstands German wartime documents. 2nd ed., 226 pages, b&w illustrations, glossary bibliography, index. (#14)

Auschwitz: Technique and Operation of the Gas Chambers: An Introduction and Update.

By Germar Rudolf. Pressac's 1989 oversize book of the same title was a trail blazer. Its many document reproductions are still valuable, but after decades of additional research, Pressac's annotations are outdated. This book summarizes the most pertinent research results on Auschwitz gained during the past 30 years. With many references to Pressac's epic tome, it serves as an update and correction to it, whether you own an original hard copy of it, read it online, borrow it from a library, purchase a reprint, or are just interested in such a summary in general. 144 pages, b&w illustrations, bibliography. (#42)

The Chemistry of Auschwitz: The Technology and Toxicology of Zyklon B and the Gas Chambers – A Crime-Scene Investigation.

By Germar Rudolf. This study documents forensic research on Auschwitz, where material traces and their interpretation reign supreme. Most of the claimed crime scenes – the claimed homicidal gas chambers – are still accessible to forensic examination to some degree. This book addresses questions such as: How were these gas chambers configured? How did they operate? In addition, the infamous Zyklon B can also be examined. What exactly was it? How does it kill? Does it leave traces in masonry that can be found still today? The author also discusses in depth similar forensic research conducted by other scholars. 4th ed., 454 pages, more than 120 color and over 100 b&w illustrations, bibliography, index. (#2)

Auschwitz Lies: Legends, Lies and Prejudices on the Holocaust.

By Carlo Mattogno and Germar Rudolf. The fallacious research and alleged "refutation" of Revisionist scholars by French biochemist G. Wellers (attacking Leuchter's famous report), Polish chemist Dr. J. Markiewicz and U.S. chemist Dr. Richard Green (taking on Rudolf's chemical research), Dr. John Zimmerman (tackling Mattogno on cremation issues), Michael Shermer and Alex Grobman (trying to prove it all), as well as researchers Keren, McCarthy and Mazal (who turned cracks into architectural features), are exposed for what they are: blatant and easily exposed political lies created to ostracize dissident historians. 4th ed., 420 pages, b&w illustrations, index. (#18)

Auschwitz: The Central Construction Office.

By Carlo Mattogno. Ever since the Russian authorities granted western historians access to their state archives in the early 1990s, the files of the Central Construction Office of the Waffen-SS and Police Auschwitz, stored in a Moscow archive, have attracted the attention of scholars who are researching the history of this most infamous of all German war-time camps. Despite this interest, next to nothing has really been known so far about this very important office, which was responsible for the planning and construction of the Auschwitz camp complex, including the crematories which are said to have contained the "gas chambers." This emphasizes the importance of the present study, which not only sheds light into this hitherto hidden

aspect of this camp's history, but also provides a deep understanding of the organization, tasks, and procedures of this office. 2nd ed., 188 pages, b&w illustrations, glossary, index. (#13)

Garrison and Headquarters Orders of the Auschwitz Camp.
By Germar Rudolf and Ernst Böhm. A large number of all the orders ever issued by the various commanders of the infamous Auschwitz camp have been preserved. They reveal the true nature of the camp with all its daily events. There is not a trace in these orders pointing at anything sinister going on in this camp. Quite to the contrary, many orders are in clear and insurmountable contradiction to claims that prisoners were mass murdered, such as the children of SS men playing with inmates, SS men taking friends for a sight-seeing tour through the camp, or having a romantic stroll with their lovers around the camp grounds. This is a selection of the most pertinent of these orders together with comments putting them into their proper historical context. 185 pages, b&w ill., bibl., index (#34)

Special Treatment in Auschwitz: Origin and Meaning of a Term.
By Carlo Mattogno. When appearing in German wartime documents, terms like "special treatment," "special action," and others have been interpreted as code words for mass murder. But that is not always true. This study focuses on documents about Auschwitz, showing that, while "special" had many different meanings, not a single one meant "execution." Hence the practice of deciphering an alleged "code language" by assigning homicidal meaning to harmless documents – a key component of mainstream historiography – is untenable. 2nd ed., 166 pages, b&w illustrations, bibliography, index. (#10)

Healthcare at Auschwitz.
By Carlo Mattogno. In extension of the above study on *Special Treatment in Auschwitz*, this study proves the extent to which the German authorities at Auschwitz tried to provide health care for the inmates. Part 1 of this book analyzes the inmates' living conditions and the various sanitary and medical measures implemented. Part 2 explores what happened to registered inmates who were "selected" or subject to "special treatment" while disabled or sick. This study shows that a lot was tried to cure these inmates, especially under the aegis of Garrison Physician Dr. Wirths. Part 3 is dedicated to this very Dr. Wirths. His reality refutes the current stereotype

of SS officers. 398 pages, b&w illustrations, bibliography, index. (#33)

Debunking the Bunkers of Auschwitz: Black Propaganda vs. History.
By Carlo Mattogno. The "bunkers" at Auschwitz, two former farmhouses just outside the camp's perimeter, are claimed to have been the first homicidal gas chambers at Auschwitz specifically equipped for this purpose. With the help of original German wartime files as well as revealing air photos taken by Allied reconnaissance aircraft in 1944, this study shows that these homicidal "bunkers" never existed, how the rumors about them evolved as black propaganda created by resistance groups in the camp, and how this propaganda was transformed into a false reality. 2nd ed., 292 pages, b&w ill., bibliography, index. (#11)

Auschwitz: The First Gassing. Rumor and Reality.
By Carlo Mattogno. The first gassing in Auschwitz is claimed to have occurred on Sept. 3, 1941 in a basement. The accounts reporting it are the archetypes for all later gassing accounts. This study analyzes all available sources about this alleged event. It shows that these sources contradict each other about the event's location, date, the kind of victims and their number, and many more aspects, which makes it impossible to extract a consistent story. Original wartime documents inflict a final blow to this legend and prove without a shadow of a doubt that this legendary event never happened. 3rd ed., 190 pages, b&w illustrations, bibliography, index. (#20)

Auschwitz: Crematorium I and the Alleged Homicidal Gassings.
By Carlo Mattogno. The morgue of Crematorium I in Auschwitz is said to be the first homicidal gas chamber there. This study investigates all statements by witnesses and analyzes hundreds of wartime documents to accurately write a history of that building. Where witnesses speak of gassings, they are either very vague or, if specific, contradict one another and are refuted by documented and material facts. The author also exposes the fraudulent attempts of mainstream historians to convert the witnesses' black propaganda into "truth" by means of selective quotes, omissions, and distortions. Mattogno proves that this building's morgue was never a homicidal gas chamber, nor could it have worked as such. 2nd ed., 152 pages, b&w illustrations, bibliography, index. (#21)

Auschwitz: Open-Air Incinerations. By Carlo Mattogno. In spring and summer of 1944, 400,000 Hungarian Jews were deported to Auschwitz and allegedly murdered there in gas chambers. The Auschwitz crematoria are said to have been unable to cope with so many corpses. Therefore, every single day thousands of corpses are claimed to have been incinerated on huge pyres lit in deep trenches. The sky over Auschwitz was filled with thick smoke. This is what some witnesses want us to believe. This book examines the many testimonies regarding these incinerations and establishes whether these claims were even possible. Using air photos, physical evidence and wartime documents, the author shows that these claims are fiction. A new Appendix contains 3 papers on groundwater levels and cattle mass burnings. 2nd ed., 202 pages, b&w illustrations, bibliography, index. (#17)

The Cremation Furnaces of Auschwitz. By Carlo Mattogno & Franco Deana. An exhaustive study of the early history and technology of cremation in general and of the cremation furnaces of Auschwitz in particular. On a vast base of technical literature, extant wartime documents and material traces, the authors can establish the true nature and capacity of the Auschwitz cremation furnaces. They show that these devices were inferior makeshift versions of what was usually produced, and that their capacity to cremate corpses was lower than normal, too. This demonstrates that the Auschwitz crematoria were not evil facilities of mass destruction, but normal installations that barely managed to handle the victims among the inmates who died of various epidemics ravaging the camp throught its history. 3 vols., 1198 pages, b&w and color illustrations (vols 2 & 3), bibliography, index, glossary. (#24)

Curated Lies: The Auschwitz Museum's Misrepresentations, Distortions and Deceptions. By Carlo Mattogno. Revisionist research results have put the Polish Auschwitz Museum under pressure to answer this challenge. In 2014, they answered with a book presenting documents allegedly proving their claims. But they cheated. In its main section, this study analyzes their "evidence" and reveals the appallingly mendacious attitude of the Auschwitz Museum authorities when presenting documents from their archives. This is preceded by a section focusing on the Auschwitz Museum's most-coveted asset: the alleged gas chamber inside the Old Crematorium, toured every year by well over a million visitors. *Curated Lies* exposes the many ways in which visitors have been deceived and misled by forgeries and misrepresentations about this building committed by the Auschwitz Museum, some of which are maintained to this day. 2nd ed., 259 pages, b&w illustrations, bibliography, index. (#38)

Deliveries of Coke, Wood and Zyklon B to Auschwitz: Neither Proof Nor Trace for the Holocaust. By Carlo Mattogno. Researchers from the Auschwitz Museum tried to prove the reality of mass extermination by pointing to documents about deliveries of wood and coke as well as Zyklon B to the Auschwitz Camp. If put into the actual historical and technical context, however, as is done by this study, these documents prove the exact opposite of what those orthodox researchers claim. 184 pages, b&w illust., bibl., index. (#40)

SECTION FOUR:
Witness Critique

Elie Wiesel, Saint of the Holocaust: A Critical Biography. By Warren B. Routledge. The world's first independent biography of Elie Wiesel shines the light of truth on this mythomaniac who has transformed the word "Holocaust" into the brand name of the world's greatest hoax. Here, both Wiesel's personal deceits and the whole myth of "the six million" are laid bare for the reader's perusal. It shows how Zionist control of the U.S. Government as well as the nation's media and academic apparatus has allowed Wiesel and his fellow extremists to force a string of U.S. presidents to genuflect before this imposter as symbolic acts of subordination to World Jewry, while simultaneously forcing school children to submit to Holocaust brainwashing by their teachers. 3rd ed., 458 pages, b&w illustration, bibliography, index. (#30)

Auschwitz: Eyewitness Reports and Perpetrator Confessions. By Jürgen Graf. The traditional narrative of what transpired at the infamous Auschwitz Camp during WWII rests almost exclusively on witness testimony. This study critically scrutinizes the 30 most-important of them by checking them for internal coherence, and by comparing them with one another as well as with other evidence such as wartime documents, air photos, forensic research results, and material traces. The result is devastating for the traditional narrative. 372 pages, b&w illust., bibl., index. (#36)

Commandant of Auschwitz: Rudolf Höss, His Torture and His Forced Confessions. By Carlo Mattogno & Rudolf Höss. From 1940 to 1943, Rudolf Höss was the commandant of the infamous Auschwitz Camp. After the war, he was captured by the British. In the following 13 months until his execution, he made 85 depositions of various kinds in which he confessed his involvement in the "Holocaust." This study first reveals how the British tortured him to extract various "confessions." Next, all of Höss's depositions are analyzed by checking his claims for internal consistency and comparing them with established historical facts. The results are eye-opening... 2nd ed., 411 pages, b&w illustrations, bibliography, index. (#35)

An Auschwitz Doctor's Eyewitness Account: The Tall Tales of Dr. Mengele's Assistant Analyzed. By Miklos Nyiszli & Carlo Mattogno. Nyiszli, a Hungarian physician, ended up at Auschwitz in 1944 as Dr. Mengele's assistant. After the war he wrote a book and several other writings describing what he claimed to have experienced. To this day some traditional historians take his accounts seriously, while others reject them as grotesque lies and exaggerations. This study presents and analyzes Nyiszli's writings and skillfully separates truth from fabulous fabrication. 2nd ed., 484 pages, b&w illustrations, bibliography, index. (#37)

Rudolf Reder versus Kurt Gerstein: Two False Testimonies on the Bełżec Camp Analyzed. By Carlo Mattogno. Only two witnesses have ever testified substantially about the alleged Belzec Extermination Camp: The survivor Rudolf Reder and the SS officer Kurt Gerstein. Gerstein's testimonies have been a hotspot of revisionist critique for decades. It is now discredited even among orthodox historians. They use Reder's testimony to fill the void, yet his testimonies are just as absurd. This study thoroughly scrutinizes Reder's various statements, critically revisits Gerstein's various depositions, and then compares these two testimonies which are at once similar in some respects, but incompatible in others. 216 pages, b&w illustrations, bibliography, index. (#43)

Sonderkommando Auschwitz I: Nine Eyewitness Testimonies Analyzed. By Carlo Mattogno. To this day, the 1979 book *Auschwitz Inferno* by former Auschwitz inmate and alleged *Sonderkommando* member Filip Müller has a great influence both on the public perception of Auschwitz and on historians trying to probe this camp's history. This book critically analyzes Müller's various post-war statements, which are full of exaggerations, falsehoods and plagiarized text passages. The author also scrutinizes the testimonies of eight other former *Sonderkommando* members with similarly lacking penchants for exactitude and truth: Dov Paisikovic, Stanisław Jankowski, Henryk Mandelbaum, Ludwik Nagraba, Joshuah Rosenblum, Aaron Pilo, David Fliamenbaum and Samij Karolinskij. 300 pages, b&w illust., bibliography, index. (#44)

Future Projects

The following projects are in various stages of research/writing/editing/translation. The titles listed and the contents summarized are tentative. These projects do not have timelines yet:

The Dachau Concentration Camp. By Carlo Mattogno. Dachau is one of the most-notorious Third-Reich camps. It's about time revisionists gave it their full attention.

Sonderkommando Auschwitz II: The False Testimonies by Henryk Tauber and Szlama Dragon. By Carlo Mattogno. These two witnesses are held in high esteem among the orthodoxy for their tales about Auschwitz: Tauber on Crema II and Dragon on the "bunkers." This study dispels the notion that these witnesses' tales are worth any more than the paper they are written on.

The "Aktion Reinhardt" Camps Bełżec, Sobibór, Treblinka: Black Propaganda, Archeological Research, Material Evidence. By Carlo Mattogno. The existing three books of the present series on each camp are all outdated, but updating them would lead to much overlap. Hence a new book with all the new insights.

Mis-Chronicling Auschwitz: Danuta Czech's Flawed Methods, Misrepresentations and Deceptions in Her Auschwitz Chronicle. By Carlo Mattogno. Danuta Czech's *Auschwitz Chronicle* is a reference book for the history of Auschwitz. Mattogno has compiled a long list of misrepresentations, outright lies and deceptions contained in it. This mega-fraud needs to be retired from the ranks of Auschwitz sources.

For current prices and availability, and to learn more, go to www.HolocaustHandbooks.com – by simply scanning the QR code to the left. Published by Castle Hill Publishers, PO Box 243, Uckfield, TN22 9AW, UK

BOOKS BY AND FROM CASTLE HILL PUBLISHERS

Below please find some of the books published or distributed by Castle Hill Publishers in the United Kingdom. For our current and complete range of products visit our web store at shop.codoh.com.

Thomas Dalton, *The Holocaust: An Introduction*

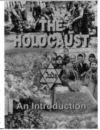

The Holocaust was perhaps the greatest crime of the 20th Century. Six million Jews, we are told, died by gassing, shooting, and deprivation. But: Where did the six-million figure come from? How, exactly, did the gas chambers work? Why do we have so little physical evidence from major death camps? Why haven't we found even a fraction of the six million bodies, or their ashes? Why has there been so much media suppression and governmental censorship on this topic? In a sense, the Holocaust is the greatest murder mystery in history. It is a topic of greatest importance for the present day. Let's explore the evidence, and see where it leads.   **128 pp. pb, 5"×8", ill., bibl., index**

Carlo Mattogno, *Auschwitz: A Three-Quarter Century of Propaganda:* *Origins, Development and Decline of the "Gas Chamber" Propaganda Lie*

During the war, wild rumors were circulating about Auschwitz: that the Germans were testing new war gases; that inmates were murdered in electrocution chambers, with gas showers or pneumatic hammer systems; that living people were sent on conveyor belts directly into cremation furnaces; that oils, grease and soap were made of the mass-murder victims. Nothing of it was true. When the Soviets captured Auschwitz in early 1945, they reported that 4 million inmates were killed on electrocution conveyor belts discharging their load directly into furnaces. That wasn't true either. After the war, "witnesses" and "experts" repeated these things and added more fantasies: mass murder with gas bombs, gas chambers made of canvas; carts driving living people into furnaces; that the crematoria of Auschwitz could have cremated 400 million victims… Again, none of it was true. This book gives an overview of the many rumors, myths and lies about Auschwitz which mainstream historians today reject as untrue. It then explains by which ridiculous methods some claims about Auschwitz were accepted as true and turned into "history," although they are just as untrue.   **125 pp. pb, 5"×8", ill., bibl., index, b&w ill.**

Wilhelm Stäglich, *Auschwitz: A Judge Looks at the Evidence*

Auschwitz is the epicenter of the Holocaust, where more people are said to have been murdered than anywhere else. At this detention camp the industrialized Nazi mass murder is said to have reached its demonic pinnacle. This narrative is based on a wide range of evidence, the most important of which was presented during two trials: the International Military Tribunal of 1945/46, and the German Auschwitz Trial of 1963-1965 in Frankfurt.

The late Wilhelm Stäglich, until the mid-1970s a German judge, has so far been the only legal expert to critically analyze this evidence. His research reveals the incredibly scandalous way in which the Allied victors and later the German judicial authorities bent and broke the law in order to come to politically foregone conclusions. Stäglich also exposes the shockingly superficial way in which historians are dealing with the many incongruities and discrepancies of the historical record.

3rd edition 2015, 422 pp. pb, 6"×9", b&w ill.

Gerard Menuhin: *Tell the Truth & Shame the Devil*

A prominent Jew from a famous family says the "Holocaust" is a wartime propaganda myth which has turned into an extortion racket. Far from bearing the sole guilt for starting WWII as alleged at Nuremberg (for which many of the surviving German leaders were hanged) Germany is mostly innocent in this respect and made numerous attempts to avoid and later to end the confrontation. During the 1930s Germany was confronted by a powerful Jewish-dominated world plutocracy out to destroy it… Yes, a prominent Jew says all this. Accept it or reject it, but be sure to read it and judge for yourself! The author is the son of the great American-born violinist Yehudi Menuhin, who, though from a long line of rabbinical ancestors, fiercely criticized the foreign policy of the state of Israel and its repression of the Palestinians in the Holy Land.

4th edition 2017, 432 pp. pb, 6"×9", b&w ill.

For prices and availability see www.shop.codoh.com or write to: CHP, PO Box 243, Uckfield, TN22 9AW, UK

Robert H. Countess, Christian Lindtner, Germar Rudolf (eds.),
Exactitude: Festschrift for Prof. Dr. Robert Faurisson

On January 25, 1929, a man was born who probably deserves the title of the most-courageous intellectual of the 20th Century and the early 21st Century: Robert Faurisson. With bravery and steadfastness, he challenged the dark forces of historical and political fraud with his unrelenting exposure of their lies and hoaxes surrounding the orthodox Holocaust narrative. This book describes and celebrates the man, who passed away on October 21, 2018, and his work dedicated to accuracy and marked by insubmission.

146 pp. pb, 6"×9", b&w ill.

Cyrus Cox, *Auschwitz – Forensically Examined*

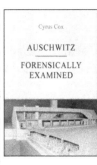

It is amazing what modern forensic crime-scene investigations can reveal. This is also true for the Holocaust. There are many big tomes about this, such as Rudolf's 400+ page book on *The Chemistry of Auschwitz*, or Mattogno's 1200-page work on the crematoria of Auschwitz. But who reads those doorstops? Here is a booklet that condenses the most-important findings of Auschwitz forensics into a nutshell, quick and easy to read. In the first section, the forensic investigations conducted so far are reviewed. In the second section, the most-important results of these studies are summarized, making them accessible to everyone. The main arguments focus on two topics. The first centers around the poison allegedly used at Auschwitz for mass murder: Zyklon B. Did it leave any traces in masonry where it was used? Can it be detected to this day? The second topic deals with mass cremations. Did the crematoria of Auschwitz have the claimed huge capacity claimed for them? Do air photos taken during the war confirm witness statements on huge smoking pyres? Find the answers to these questions in this booklet, together with many references to source material and further reading. The third section reports on how the establishment has reacted to these research results.

124 pp. pb., 5"×8", b&w ill., bibl., index

Steffen Werner, *The Second Babylonian Captivity:* The Fate of the Jews in Eastern Europe since 1941

"But if they were not murdered, where did the six million deported Jews end up?" This is a standard objection to the revisionist thesis that the Jews were not killed in extermination camps. It demands a well-founded response. While researching an entirely different topic, Steffen Werner accidentally stumbled upon the most-peculiar demographic data of Byelorussia. Years of research subsequently revealed more and more evidence which eventually allowed him to substantiate a breathtaking and sensational proposition: The Third Reich did indeed deport many of the Jews of Europe to Eastern Europe in order to settle them there "in the swamp." This book, first published in German in 1990, was the first well-founded work showing what really happened to the Jews deported to the East by the National Socialists, how they have fared since, and who, what and where they are "now" (1990). It provides context and purpose for hitherto-obscure and seemingly random historical events and quite obviates all need for paranormal events such as genocide, gas chambers, and all their attendant horrifics. With a preface by Germar Rudolf with references to more-recent research results in this field of study confirming Werner's thesis.

190 pp. pb, 6"×9", b&w ill., bibl., index

Germar Rudolf, *Holocaust Skepticism:* 20 Questions and Answers about Holocaust Revisionism

This 15-page brochure introduces the novice to the concept of Holocaust revisionism, and answers 20 tough questions, among them: What does Holocaust revisionism claim? Why should I take Holocaust revisionism more seriously than the claim that the earth is flat? How about the testimonies by survivors and confessions by perpetrators? What about the pictures of corpse piles in the camps? Why does it matter how many Jews were killed by the Nazis, since even 1,000 would have been too many? ... Glossy full-color brochure. PDF file free of charge available at www.HolocaustHandbooks.com, Option "Promotion". This item is *not* copyright-protected. Hence, you can do with it whatever you want: download, post, email, print, multiply, hand out, sell...

15 pp., stapled, 8.5"×11", full-color throughout

For prices and availability see www.shop.codoh.com or write to: CHP, PO Box 243, Uckfield, TN22 9AW, UK

Germar Rudolf, *Bungled: "Denying the Holocaust"* How Deborah Lipstadt Botched *Her Attempt to Demonstrate the Growing Assault on Truth and Memory*

With her book *Denying the Holocaust*, Deborah Lipstadt tried to show the flawed methods and extremist motives of "Holocaust deniers." This book demonstrates that Dr. Lipstadt clearly has neither understood the principles of science and scholarship, nor has she any clue about the historical topics she is writing about. She misquotes, mistranslates, misrepresents, misinterprets, and makes a plethora of wild claims without backing them up with anything. Rather than dealing thoroughly with factual arguments, Lipstadt's book is full of *ad hominem* attacks on her opponents. It is an exercise in anti-intellectual pseudo-scientific arguments, an exhibition of ideological radicalism that rejects anything which contradicts its preset conclusions. **F for FAIL**

2nd ed., 224 pp. pb, 5"×8", bibl., index, b&w ill.

Carolus Magnus, *Bungled: "Denying History"*. *How Michael Shermer and Alex Grobman Botched Their Attempt to Refute Those Who Say the Holocaust Never Happened*

Skeptic Magazine editor Michael Shermer and Alex Grobman from the Simon Wiesenthal Center wrote a book in 2000 which they claim is "a thorough and thoughtful answer to all the claims of the Holocaust deniers." In 2009, a new "updated" edition appeared with the same ambitious goal. In the meantime, revisionists had published some 10,000 pages of archival and forensic research results. Would their updated edition indeed answer all the revisionist claims? In fact, Shermer and Grobman completely ignored the vast amount of recent scholarly studies and piled up a heap of falsifications, contortions, omissions, and fallacious interpretations of the evidence. Finally, what the authors claim to have demolished is not revisionism but a ridiculous parody of it. They ignored the known unreliability of their cherry-picked selection of evidence, utilizing unverified and incestuous sources, and obscuring the massive body of research and all the evidence that dooms their project to failure. **F for FAIL**

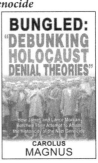

162 pp. pb, 5"×8", bibl., index, b&w ill.

Carolus Magnus, *Bungled: "Debunking Holocaust Denial Theories"*. *How James and Lance Morcan Botched Their Attempt to Affirm the Historicity of the Nazi Genocide*

The novelists and movie-makers James and Lance Morcan have produced a book "to end [Holocaust] denial once and for all." To do this, "no stone was left unturned" to verify historical assertions by presenting "a wide array of sources" meant "to shut down the debate deniers wish to create." One by one, the various arguments Holocaust deniers use to try to discredit wartime records are carefully scrutinized and then systematically disproven." It's a lie. First, the Morcans completely ignored the vast amount of recent scholarly studies published by revisionists; they didn't even mention them. Instead, they engaged in shadowboxing, creating some imaginary, bogus "revisionist" scarecrow which they then tore to pieces. In addition, their knowledge even of their own side's source material was dismal, and the way they backed up their misleading or false claims was pitifully inadequate. **F for FAIL.**

144 pp. pb, 5"×8", bibl., index, b&w ill.

Joachim Hoffmann, *Stalin's War of Extermination 1941-1945*

A German government historian documents Stalin's murderous war against the German army and the German people. Based on the author's lifelong study of German and Russian military records, this book reveals the Red Army's grisly record of atrocities against soldiers and civilians, as ordered by Stalin. Since the 1920s, Stalin planned to invade Western Europe to initiate the "World Revolution." He prepared an attack which was unparalleled in history. The Germans noticed Stalin's aggressive intentions, but they underestimated the strength of the Red Army. What unfolded was the cruelest war in history. This book shows how Stalin and his Bolshevik henchman used unimaginable violence and atrocities to break any resistance in the Red Army and to force their unwilling soldiers to fight against the Germans. The book explains how Soviet propagandists incited their soldiers to unlimited hatred against everything German, and he gives the reader a short but extremely unpleasant glimpse into what happened when these Soviet soldiers finally reached German soil in 1945: A gigantic wave of looting, arson, rape, torture, and mass murder...

428 pp. pb, 6"×9", bibl., index, b&w ill.

For prices and availability see www.shop.codoh.com or write to: CHP, PO Box 243, Uckfield, TN22 9AW, UK

Udo Walendy, *Who Started World War II: Truth for a War-Torn World*

For seven decades, mainstream historians have insisted that Germany was the main, if not the sole culprit for unleashing World War II in Europe. In the present book this myth is refuted. There is available to the public today a great number of documents on the foreign policies of the Great Powers before September 1939 as well as a wealth of literature in the form of memoirs of the persons directly involved in the decisions that led to the outbreak of World War II. Together, they made possible Walendy's present mosaic-like reconstruction of the events before the outbreak of the war in 1939. This book has been published only after an intensive study of sources, taking the greatest care to minimize speculation and inference. The present edition has been translated completely anew from the German original and has been slightly revised.

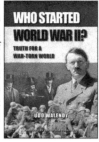

500 pp. pb, 6"×9", index, bibl., b&w ill.

Germar Rudolf: *Resistance Is Obligatory!*

In 2005 Rudolf, a peaceful dissident and publisher of revisionist literature, was kidnapped by the U.S. government and deported to Germany. There the local lackey regime staged a show trial against him for his historical writings. Rudolf was not permitted to defend his historical opinions, as the German penal law prohibits this. Yet he defended himself anyway: For 7 full days Rudolf gave a speech in the courtroom, during which he proved systematically that only the revisionists are scholarly in their approach, whereas the Holocaust orthodoxy is merely pseudo-scientific. He then explained in detail why it is everyone's obligation to resist, without violence, a government which throws peaceful dissidents into dungeons. When Rudolf tried to publish his public defence speech as a book from his prison cell, the public prosecutor initiated a new criminal investigation against him. After his probation time ended in 2011, he dared publish this speech anyway...

2nd ed. 2016, 378 pp. pb, 6"×9", b&w ill.

Germar Rudolf, *Hunting Germar Rudolf: Essays on a Modern-Day Witch Hunt*

German-born revisionist activist, author and publisher Germar Rudolf describes which events made him convert from a Holocaust believer to a Holocaust skeptic, quickly rising to a leading personality within the revisionist movement. This in turn unleashed a tsunami of persecution against him: lost his job, denied his PhD exam, destruction of his family, driven into exile, slandered by the mass media, literally hunted, caught, put on a show trial where filing motions to introduce evidence is illegal under the threat of further prosecution, and finally locked up in prison for years for nothing else than his peaceful yet controversial scholarly writings. In several essays, Rudolf takes the reader on a journey through an absurd world of government and societal persecution which most of us could never even fathom actually exists in a "Western democracy"....

304 pp. pb, 6"×9", bibl., index, b&w ill.

Germar Rudolf, *The Day Amazon Murdered History*

Amazon is the world's biggest book retailer. They dominate the U.S. and several foreign markets. Pursuant to the 1998 declaration of Amazon's founder Jeff Bezos to offer "the good, the bad and the ugly," customers once could buy every title that was in print and was legal to sell. However, in early 2017, a series of anonymous bomb threats against Jewish community centers occurred in the U.S., fueling a campaign by Jewish groups to coax Amazon into banning revisionist writings, falsely portraying them as anti-Semitic. On March 6, 2017, Amazon caved in and banned more than 100 books with dissenting viewpoints on the Holocaust. In April 2017, an Israeli Jew was arrested for having placed the fake bomb threats, a paid "service" he had offered for years. But that did not change Amazon's policy. Its stores remain closed for history books Jewish lobby groups disapprove of. This book accompanies the documentary of the same title. Both reveal how revisionist publications had become so powerfully convincing that the powers that be resorted to what looks like a dirty false-flag operation in order to get these books banned from Amazon...

128 pp. pb, 5"×8", bibl., b&w ill.

For prices and availability see www.shop.codoh.com or write to: CHP, PO Box 243, Uckfield, TN22 9AW, UK

Thomas Dalton, *Hitler on the Jews*

That Adolf Hitler spoke out against the Jews is beyond obvious. But of the thousands of books and articles written on Hitler, virtually none quotes Hitler's exact words on the Jews. The reason for this is clear: Those in positions of influence have incentives to present a simplistic picture of Hitler as a blood-thirsty tyrant. However, Hitler's take on the Jews is far more complex and sophisticated. In this book, for the first time, you can make up your own mind by reading nearly every idea that Hitler put forth about the Jews, in considerable detail and in full context. This is the first book ever to compile his remarks on the Jews. As you will discover, Hitler's analysis of the Jews, though hostile, is erudite, detailed, and – surprise, surprise – largely aligns with events of recent decades. There are many lessons here for the modern-day world to learn.

200 pp. pb, 6"×9", index, bibl.

Thomas Dalton, *Goebbels on the Jews*

From the age of 26 until his death in 1945, Joseph Goebbels kept a near-daily diary. From it, we get a detailed look at the attitudes of one of the highest-ranking men in Nazi Germany. Goebbels shared Hitler's dislike of the Jews, and likewise wanted them totally removed from the Reich territory. Ultimately, Goebbels and others sought to remove the Jews completely from the Eurasian land mass—perhaps to the island of Madagascar. This would be the "final solution" to the Jewish Question. Nowhere in the diary does Goebbels discuss any Hitler order to kill the Jews, nor is there any reference to extermination camps, gas chambers, or any methods of systematic mass-murder. Goebbels acknowledges that Jews did indeed die by the thousands; but the range and scope of killings evidently fall far short of the claimed figure of 6 million. This book contains, for the first time, every significant diary entry relating to the Jews or Jewish policy. Also included are partial or full transcripts of 10 major essays by Goebbels on the Jews.

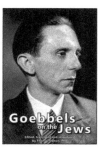

274 pp. pb, 6"×9", index, bibl.

Thomas Dalton, *The Jewish Hand in the World Wars*

For many centuries, Jews have had a negative reputation in many countries. The reasons given are plentiful, but less-well-known is their involvement in war. When we examine the causal factors for wars, and look at their primary beneficiaries, we repeatedly find a Jewish presence. Throughout history, Jews have played an exceptionally active role in promoting and inciting wars. With their long-notorious influence in government, we find recurrent instances of Jews promoting hard-line stances, being uncompromising, and actively inciting people to hatred. Jewish misanthropy, rooted in Old Testament mandates, and combined with a ruthless materialism, has led them, time and again, to instigate warfare if it served their larger interests. This fact explains much about the present-day world. In this book, Thomas Dalton examines in detail the Jewish hand in the two world wars. Along the way, he dissects Jewish motives and Jewish strategies for maximizing gain amidst warfare, reaching back centuries.

197 pp. pb, 6"×9", index, bibl.

Thomas Dalton, *Eternal Strangers: Critical Views of Jews and Judaism through the Ages*

It is common knowledge that Jews have been disliked for centuries. But why? Our best hope for understanding this recurrent 'anti-Semitism' is to study the history: to look at the actual words written by prominent critics of the Jews, in context, and with an eye to any common patterns that might emerge. Such a study reveals strikingly consistent observations: Jews are seen in very negative, yet always similar terms. The persistence of such comments is remarkable and strongly suggests that the cause for such animosity resides in the Jews themselves—in their attitudes, their values, their ethnic traits and their beliefs.. This book addresses the modern-day "Jewish problem" in all its depth—something which is arguably at the root of many of the world's social, political and economic problems.

186 pp. pb, 6"×9", index, bibl.

Thomas Dalton, *Streicher, Rosenberg, and the Jews: The Nuremberg Transcripts*

Who, apart from Hitler, contrived the Nazi view on the Jews? And what were these master ideologues thinking? During the post-war International Military Tribunal at Nuremberg, the most-interesting men on trial

For prices and availability see www.shop.codoh.com or write to: CHP, PO Box 243, Uckfield, TN22 9AW, UK

regarding this question were two with a special connection to the "Jewish Question": Alfred Rosenberg and Julius Streicher. The cases against them, and their personal testimonies, examined for the first time nearly all major aspects of the Holocaust story: the "extermination" thesis, the gas chambers, the gas vans, the shootings in the East, and the "6 million." The truth of the Holocaust has been badly distorted for decades by the powers that be. Here we have the rare opportunity to hear firsthand from two prominent figures in Nazi Germany. Their voices, and their verbatim transcripts from the IMT, lend some much-needed clarity to the situation.

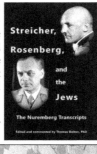

330 pp. pb, 6"×9", index, bibl.

The Queen versus Zündel: *The First Zündel Trial: The Transcript*

In the early 1980s, Ernst Zündel, a German immigrant living in Toronto, was indicted for allegedly spreading "false news" by selling copies of Richard Harwood's brochure *Did Six Million Really Die?*, which challenged the accuracy of the orthodox Holocaust narrative. When the case went to court in 1985, so-called Holocaust experts and "eyewitnesses" of the alleged homicidal gas chambers at Auschwitz were cross-examined for the first time in history by a competent and skeptical legal team. The results were absolutely devastating for the Holocaust orthodoxy. Even the prosecutor, who had summoned these witnesses to bolster the mainstream Holocaust narrative, became at times annoyed by their incompetence and mendacity. For decades, these mind-boggling trial transcripts were hidden from public view. Now, for the first time, they have been published in print in this new book – unabridged and unedited.

820 pp. pb, 8.5"×11"

Barbara Kulaszka (ed.), *The Second Zündel Trial: Excerpts from the Transcript*

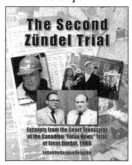

In 1988. German-Canadian Ernst Zündel was on trial for a second time for allegedly spreading "false news" about the Holocaust. Zündel staged a magnificent defense in an attempt to prove that revisionist concepts of "the Holocaust" are essentially correct. Although many of the key players have since passed away, including Zündel, this historic trial keeps having an impact. It inspired major research efforts as expounded in the series *Holocaust Handbooks*. In contrast to the First Zündel Trial of 1985, the second trial had a much greater impact internationally, mainly due to the **Leuchter Report**, the first independent forensic research performed on Auschwitz, which was endorsed on the witness stand by British bestselling historian David Irving. The present book features the essential contents of this landmark trial with all the gripping, at-times-dramatic details. When Amazon.com decided to ban this 1992 book on a landmark trial about the "Holocaust", we decided to put it back in print, lest censorship prevail…

498 pp. pb, 8.5"×11", bibl., index, b&w ill.

Gerard Menuhin: *Lies & Gravy: Landmarks in Human Decay – Two Plays*

A long time ago, in a galaxy far, far away, the hallucination of global supremacy was born. Few paid it any attention. After centuries of interference, when the end is in sight, we're more inclined to take it seriously. But now, we have only a few years of comparative freedom left before serfdom submerges us all. So it's time to summarize our fall and to name the guilty, or, as some have it, to spot the loony. Sometimes the message is so dire that the only way to get it across is with humor – to act out our predicament and its causes. No amount of expert testimony can match the power of spectacle. Here are a few of the most-telling stages in the chosenites' crusade against humanity, and their consequences, as imagined by the author. We wonder whether these two consecutive plays will ever be performed onstage…

112 pp. pb, 5"×8"

For current prices and availability see book-finder sites such as www.findbookprices.com; learn more at https://shop.codoh.com by simply scanning the QR code to the left with you smart device.
Published by Castle Hill Publishers, PO Box 243, Uckfield, TN22 9AW, UK

CPSIA information can be obtained
at www.ICGtesting.com
Printed in the USA
BVHW031924310721
613179BV00031B/1429

9 781591 489689